WRITING MYSTERY AND CRIME FICTION

Writing Mystery and Crime Fiction

Edited by SYLVIA K. BURACK

Publishers   THE WRITER, INC.   Boston

Library of Congress Cataloging in Publication Data

Main entry under title:
Writing mystery and crime fiction.
  1. Detective and mystery stories—Technique.
I. Burack, Sylvia K.
PN3377.5.D4W68 1985   808.3′872   84-21952
ISBN 0-87116-141-9 (pbk.)

Printed in the United States of America

CONTENTS

WRITING MYSTERY AND CRIME FICTION

1 WELL BEGUN IS HALF DONE
by *Catherine Aird*

I HAVE found that one of the best ways to write a crime story is to take a situation and work out what could have led up to it. And then examine the action which subsequently arises—naturally or otherwise—from that particular situation.

In one tale that I wrote, I began with a road accident in which a widow was knocked down and killed by a car that did not stop after the accident. Her daughter is called home from college and identifies the body as that of her mother—all very routine so far. Then, after the post mortem, the hospital pathologist announces that the woman who had been killed had not only never had a baby, but had not been married either, and so could not have been the girl's mother.

Exploring the possibilities of that particular situation—working out ways it could have come about, intertwining it with the malice aforethought without which no crime writing is complete, and—of course, you've guessed it—deciding that the road death was no accident gave me enough plot to carry me to the point in the story where the action stemming from the opening came into its own.

Where then to go for the promising opening situation?

First of all it can be quite a good idea to sit down and think of all the occasions when you have said to yourself, I have always wondered why. . . ."

In everyone's experience, there are situations, apparently

inexplicable, which could well bear the close examination of the crime novelist:

The rich man who dies penniless.

The poor woman who dies very rich indeed.

The highly personable man who has never married.

The seasoned traveler and perpetual globetrotter who suddenly won't leave home.

The man who sets out quite normally for the office one morning and is never seen again.

The company executive whose early retirement is so premature as to be startling.

The erstwhile friends who now never speak to each other. . . .

In fact the list could be endless. It is, though, worth giving some thought to. I am not in any way, of course, suggesting that you should write too closely about real people: rather that you should use a real-life situation that has always puzzled you to start you thinking.

And that to start with a situation without knowing the outcome is not necessarily a bad thing. ("I distinctly remember," wrote Lewis Carroll of *Alice's Adventures in Wonderland,* "how, in a desperate attempt to strike out some new line of fairy-lore, I had sent my heroine straight down a rabbit-hole, to begin with, without the least idea what was to happen afterwards. . . .")

Newspaper sources

There is one piece of wisdom that most of the good books on how to write have in common. Almost all of them advise would-be writers to study their daily newspapers. It is there you are most likely to find the faintly, but not too, bizarre report that might give you the opening situation that you are waiting for.

One that comes immediately to mind is the not-infrequent

news item about some unstable member of a family being kept at home and out of sight for years—usually imprisoned in an attic bedroom. Now there is a promising beginning for a crime story. . . . In real life, the reasons are usually unhappy, diseased ones, but at the hands of a crime writer, the situation has great possibilities.

Beginning, perhaps, with the accidental discovery that there are, say, three people in a household that the outside world believes has only two, the story could obviously develop in a number of different ways. Ten writers could take that as the beginning and they would produce ten different novels.

Take the report of a disaster in which a great deal of insurance compensation stands to be paid out when the blame is finally laid at the culprit's door. There is a wide scope here for the disappearance or doctoring of tapes, witnesses, records, etc., and unlimited opportunity for working in background. This can be a hospital, big business, marine travel, an airport, mining—what you will.

Do not neglect the personal column of the newspaper. The imagination of every novelist is bound to be excited by the anxious advertiser who *must* trace the person who traveled in the last coach of the 6:15 p.m. train from Victoria Station and picked up a ladies' umbrella.

Now weave together all three circumstances—the incarcerated person, the big insurance payment, and the too-important umbrella—and you will have the threads of a story.

Another practical way in which a newspaper report of an international or national news story can be used by mystery writers is for them to give the story a small-town setting. This is a matter of reduction of scale—from global to local—and of changing the setting, too, but not changing the kernel of the story. If you take a major political theme and use it, suitably modified, in miniature, at the very least you will have a sturdy plot upon which to hang your dialogue and background. (Shakespeare was particularly good at doing this.)

It is well to remember that the grand passions of high life exist in villagers as well as in the jet set; that power corrupts at all levels, not just at the top; that integrity is as important in the administration of local school funds as in those of the state.

It is equally important, I think, to be aware that all crime writing is really good versus evil. Any situation that highlights this is potentially useful to the crime novelist. A logical extension of this theory would be the consideration of almost all moral dilemmas as source material. There's richness!

Another type of situation that occasionally finds its way into the newspapers is the sort of law report that everyone suspects is just the tip of an iceberg of incident, interest, and intrigue. A writer should need only the tip of an iceberg to start the imagination working and, moreover, should make a habit of letting it do so. I know that it is the counsel of perfection, but this sort of practice is useful; five-finger exercises are the recognized route to a concerto.

Exercise in plotting

If you should ever happen to listen to an interview with a concert pianist, I think you can safely count on the virtuoso of the piano's being asked how many hours a day he or she practices. Ballet dancers are said to need a day's practice for every day's rest, but exercises are seldom mentioned in the life of the aspiring writer. I think this is a pity. There are certain exercises in plot-making which I would say at the very least did no harm.

Dear to the heart of many crime writers is the locked-room mystery. The Sherlock Holmes "Speckled Band" story was one of the first in a long line of tales of victims in a room demonstrably locked on the inside, apparently without any way in or out. Perhaps every crime writer should try his or her ingenuity on how he would set about—and solve—his own locked-room mystery.

The two oldest detective stories in the world are said to be "The Tale of Susannah and the Elders" and "Bel and the Dragon," both in the *Apocrypha*. A productive exercise for a crime writer might be to try writing a modern version of each. I am sure I am not alone in thinking that Josephine Tey's book *Brat Farrar*—a marvelous crime novel—has overtones of Joseph and the pit in Dothan from *Genesis*—indeed, the author mentions it.

The great merit for a writer who does such an exercise may come either from the actual writing of the story or just from thinking about it and making notes on paper, which go into a drawer against the day when they can be used in a crime novel.

There is yet another way of seeking out something—not a situation this time—that can be the *raison d'être* of a plot. This is to take a general proposition, the more arguable the better, and use this as a basis for your whole tale.

Do you, for instance, believe that—

. . . corruption is harmful only if it is against the public interest?

. . . the research scientist owes his first duty to humanity and not to his employers?

. . . every man has his price?

. . . sons are always taller than their mothers? (This is a nice crime story beginning. A "son" who is shorter than his mother isn't her son. . . .)

. . . a stateless person need have no patriotism? (This could have interesting possibilities in the thriller/spy field.)

. . . the doctrine of "my country right or wrong" is a good one? (This isn't quite so old-fashioned when you turn it into, "My Company, right or wrong," and enter the fascinating— and by no means overworked—field of business ethics and crime.)

. . . you can't cheat an honest man? (And the more you think about that one, the more interesting the idea is.)

You may find disagreement with a particular proposition

more stimulating than concurrence. Either way, if you are "given furiously to think"—as with a situation—then you have the beginnings of a workable plot, and that, after all, is the object of the exercise.

Imagination and experience

You will observe that what I have suggested to you firstly are some pathways to opening situations, and secondly some very general ideas around which it is possible to build a plot: not, given both, the way to go on from there. This is the point at which the individual writer's own imagination and experience should come into its own.

Every writer will—must—treat each subject differently, and I am convinced that this can be done best by the author, however hard it is to do. For instance, there are a hundred ways of treating this particular crime story: A student comes home from a visit abroad to find that his father has died, and his mother is remarried to his father's brother, who has taken over the family business in the student's absence. The student is in danger from his uncle, to whom he constitutes a threat. . . .

A promising beginning? Shakespeare made *Hamlet* out of it. Denying yourself the device of the Ghost of Hamlet's Father—since we are in the twentieth century—why don't you see what you can do with this as an opening situation?

It won't be *Hamlet,* but it could be a good crime story.

2 TRICKS AND TRAPS IN WRITING SUSPENSE FICTION

by *Jean L. Backus*

DESPITE THE CRIES of some intellectual writers who often have nothing to say and say it beautifully, certain writers of suspense fiction continue to publish in a world where the market has grown increasingly crowded. Why is this? How do they manage to put out book after book which people buy eagerly and read with enthusiasm? And why is it that certain publishing writers fail when they turn to the suspense field? I think it is because they do not understand that suspense, while motivating all fiction, can be enjoyed for its own sake. A writer's ability to generate this special thrill of vicarious pain or pleasure in a reader depends on learning useful tricks and avoidable traps and applying them deliberately to any story material, right from the beginning.

The long realistic or straight novel can wind down to a quiet close if a writer wants it to, but not the suspense novel. Most of us have panted with fright as we cheered the hero or hissed the villain in a thriller, only to shut the book with a sense of disappointment because the writer has let us down with an ending of less impact than the story's problem demanded and unworthy of its development. Yet a simple trick can avoid this plotting trap. At the onset of an idea for a brilliant opening, incredible situation, fascinating character, or fabulous gimmick, the writer explores every possible ending, however un-

9

likely, and selects the one which is realistically inevitable and won't let his reader down. From the very first word, the writer will know where the plot is going and will develop the material with the single purpose of reaching that goal. Never mind if readers hate the ending; reason and logic will convince them that this particular story could end in no other way.

On the other hand, the writer who begins with a perfect ending and then must find a story to go with it has the problem of providing a good opening. The sprawling family saga may start with a character's birth, but for a suspense novel, the moment just before, or the moment which actually precipitates the action is the moment to begin the story. Often a character arrives or departs, is sent on a mission, finds a body, is accused of a crime or plans a crime. . . . The variations are many, each one designed to lure the readers from TV or any other endeavor and engross them for several hours. In addition, planting the big clue to the solution as soon as possible is a trick almost certain to guarantee the reader will be fooled but will not feel foolish or betrayed when everything becomes clear.

Before the beginning

What about events leading up to and necessary to explain this critical moment of action? Flashbacks used soon after the opening take care of them, but there is a trap inherent in flashbacks: they may put so much information into the fabric of the story that it tears holes in the continuity, stops the action, and breaks the tension of the opening. Flashbacks must be compressed and confined to information essential for understanding the threat to the character, the nature of the story problem, and/or predicting the solution. Is there a special technique or trick that can be used to give essential information without using a genuine flashback? There is: *a glancing reference.*

Sometimes this is a paragraph or two of narrative; sometimes no more than a few words in the character's thoughts or dialogue. For example, "That part of the itinerary Sheila approved heartily. She and her ex-husband had stayed at the Carlton in London a year ago. Now it would take most of her first alimony check to pay for a suite, but she deserved a celebration." Unless the ex-husband threatens Sheila or influences what will happen to her, the reader doesn't have to know much more about him. Conversely, should the ex-husband be an important influence or be destined to appear later on in the story, this type of glancing reference throughout can describe and characterize him so thoroughly that his appearance, while it may come as a surprise, will not shock the reader.

There is also the *plot step,* the small propellant that ends a scene or chapter and sends the reader urgently on to find out what happens next. The opposite of flashback, this is foreshadowing with a vengeance, sometimes a page long, sometimes only a paragraph, or even a few words, such as, "Billy heard the shots in the distance. Coming closer." Can anyone bear not to find out if the guns are coming for Billy? Often the plot step can utilize speculation by a character, a good trick for misleading the reader. For instance, "She wondered if John would be calm or violent when he came home. Violent, probably, he usually was." It is acceptable then if the character (and therefore the reader) guesses wrong and John shows up in a calm mood.

Progressive complications

With the opening and the ending of a story worked out, the writer must still avoid the trap of creating complications that are fascinating but do not pertain to the main plot or lead to the chosen solution. "Because of this, that happened . . ." is a simple phrase, but it guarantees that each complication will evolve naturally and inevitably from the one before it.

I used that formula in plotting *Traitor's Wife.* Because Neal

Borden had murdered their son, his wife Della subconsciously wanted to kill him. Because Neal defected to the USSR, she agreed to accompany Peter Wing to a rendezvous arranged for their own reasons by the Russians. Because Peter was threatened en route, he killed his Russian contact. Because this aroused doubts of his loyalty, another agent was sent to kill Peter. Because this agent tried to rape Della, she killed him in Munich. Because they had to flee from the Bavarian police . . . and so on and on, until the end. Because Peter Wing's cover as a double agent was blown, the story ended happily. Did she kill her husband as foretold in the opening? No. But she had her reasons because of . . . .

This trick is extremely useful for developing or changing a character's motivation. Every detail from bald pate to gilded toenail may be necessary to show what the character looks like, but unless the reader understands why that character reacts as he does to the complications of the story, he won't come alive or convince the reader.

Take a ballerina, for instance, like my main character in *Dusha*. Kedrovna was dedicated to her dancing and devoted to Russia. She could conceive of no reason which would induce her to defect to the West. But because she was arrested and confined in a hospital, because her lover disappeared, and because she was threatened with banishment to Siberia (although innocent of all charges), she finally decided to abandon her homeland.

There is also a trick to choosing the right viewpoint character from which to tell a suspense story. The writer must examine the story material and discover the one person who is closest to the drama, most affected by the conflict, in the greatest danger, or who holds the key to the solution. Alternatively, the writer can choose the person from whom the most information must be hidden, who must go the farthest distance in solving the problem, or expend the greatest effort to bring the story to its close. Either way, the writer will have chosen the viewpoint which best exploits the material and generates the greatest drama.

Playing upon emotions

Next to plot and character motivation, the use of emotion produces the strongest suspense. Not only should the suspense fiction writer play upon various character responses, but also upon the responses of readers—their curiosity, anticipation, and their ultimate satisfaction. Readers must be made to experience vicariously the emotions aroused by the situation and by those who live through it. The trick lies in dealing honestly and realistically with the causes and effects of every action. The trap lies in dealing lightly with serious causes, or presenting effects out of all proportion to the cause. Sentimentality or melodrama or both can result if the writer does not avoid the overuse of adverbs, especially in action scenes, and exaggerated emotional effects in dramatic clashes. If a person tosses off an assault as a joke, or regards a missed appointment as serious as finding a body, false emotion will be generated. On the other hand, the judicious use of secondary causes can build more emotion than is otherwise possible. If the intended victim of murder is already condemned by a terminal illness, the effect of threat and approaching danger is doubled. But one should be cautious about piling it on until murder looks preferable to what the character already has to contend with.

Fair—and unfair—game

Achieving credibility in suspense fiction is one of the thorniest problems for writers. Readers will suspend disbelief to a certain extent, but it's unfair to ask the impossible of them unless the writer has made the impossible appear possible. The trick for accomplishing this depends on how much value a character places on life, property, power, revenge, or whatever, and how much he will risk to preserve or acquire his objective. If a boy climbs a dangerously steep cliff under no compulsion but his own desire to rescue a lamb, his climbing the cliff later to rescue a man who is being shot at will be credible. The trap of incredibility lies either in not showing the pattern of values and risks early enough, or in not showing it at all.

Writers may mislead readers *fairly,* with misinterpretation and misjudgment, disguise and diversion, or false deductions on the part of the characters, or by introducing new evidence or additional crimes; almost anything can be used—except a lie on the part of the writer. And almost anything can be told casually to the readers, if a startling development or a compelling piece of action follows at once, because readers, to one degree or another, read in order to be misled, or perversely, to trap the writer. But readers are subject to knee-jerk reactions as well. Show a character doing something foul, and right away the reader wants to hate that person and believe him guilty of every crime imaginable. But should such a character turn out to be the good guy after all, the writer had better have a reasonable explanation for the earlier bad behavior.

In a day when readers demand real blood instead of ketchup and real sex instead of drawn curtains and three dots, a writer has to decide for himself how much or how little of either to include in a novel. The trick is for the writer to make the sex or the violent scene, or any other scene, for that matter, earn its right to be dramatized. Let that scene reveal character, project future development, hide clues or plants, or end in a conclusive decision or act, but whatever it does, make it work to advance the story. The trap is to put in a scene purely for shock value, even if it stops the action and thus ruins the pace.

In the first draft, pacing should be ignored, since inspiration should not be sacrificed to reason. Normal rewriting and revision, the deepening and expansion of motives and explanations, the dramatizing of scenes passed over, plus the removal of excess wordage, repetitions, insignificant details, irrelevancies, or any other story stopper, usually takes care of pacing. But if the story seems to move too rapidly, the trick is to add complications, delay and retard the action, insert roadblocks to the solution, always making certain these are genuine and relate to the plot line. Conversely, if the story moves too slowly, remove excessive complications, combine those which closely resemble one another, and condense and cut once again. The story will then be so taut that not a single word could be cut without destroying the whole effect.

When planning is carefully and completely thought out, when writing is honest and realistic, suspense and tension are achieved by continuity, consistency, and clarity. Readers then unaware of traps avoided and tricks used will finish the story or close the book with a genuine sigh of satisfaction and pleasure.

3

THE MAN IN THE CLOSET
by *Cecilia Bartholomew*

THE *known is more suspenseful than the unknown.* Answer
True or False. Offhand you'd say "false," wouldn't you? But
there is nothing offhand about suspense writing—which is
what we are really talking about. And, you were wrong: the
opening statement is true. Take, for instance, the man in the
closet.

What man? Well, that's just the point. You didn't see him
go into the closet. You don't know he's there. You see Marilyn
come home to her apartment with her escort. You see them say
a tender good night at the door. Jeff wants to come in for a
while, but Marilyn is a nice girl; besides, the landlord doesn't
allow male visitors after midnight, and she says a firm no. Jeff
leaves and Marilyn goes in, shuts the door, fixes the latch. She
takes off her coat, walks into the bedroom, puts her hand on
the closet door to open it, and out jumps the man.

Great stuff, you say. It made your hair stand on end. Your
heart gave a big jump and is still beating hard. You could not
wait to read on. Well, naturally, you were surprised. Nobody
said you wouldn't be surprised. The unknown does surprise; it
does shock. But we're talking about suspense. Suppose you
see the man go into the closet to hide. You know he is there!
All right, let's write it.

The apartment is empty; only one lamp is left burning.
Marilyn has gone out for an evening on the town with Jeff. In

16

the waiting silence, you see the fire escape window slowly open, and a man climbs over the sill. His precautions tip you off to the fact that he is an intruder. He hardly has time to look around the joint before you (and he) hear voices, and it is apparent that Marilyn and Jeff are returning earlier than expected. The intruder tiptoes hastily into the bedroom, jumps into the clothes closet, and closes the door just as Marilyn unlocks the front door.

It seems that our friend Jeff has been pushing things a little too fast, and Marilyn, being a nice girl, will have none of that. Jeff apologizes, says he should have known better, and won't she please give him another chance. ("Give him another chance," you hiss urgently, "Keep him around. There's a man in your closet.") Marilyn considers, decides to give him another chance. (You breathe a sigh of relief.) But not tonight, she says, tomorrow evening. ("You idiot," you shout, helplessly mute. And at the same time you're frantically coaching Jeff to charm her, to overwhelm her, to do anything that he has to do, but just stay around to protect her.) Jeff seems to catch something in the atmosphere; at any rate he hesitates, he wants to stay—but his cheek is still red. And Marilyn, innocent and a bit smug, determined to teach him a lesson, is closing the door in his face. ("All right," you mutter, "take the consequences. It's not my funeral." But the point is that you know the man is in the closet, and so in a sense it is your funeral.)

Marilyn takes off her coat and starts into the bedroom. ("Don't put it in the closet," you shout impotently. Well, thank God for small favors, she isn't one of those neat dames who have to hang up something the minute they take it off.) Marilyn drops her coat on the couch and goes toward the kitchen, but on the way, she notices the open window. You can see her thinking, did she leave it open? ("Of course you didn't," you warn her. "Think! What does an open window mean? Go for help!") But instead, she merely closes the window and goes for a glass of milk. (While she's at the refrigera-

tor, you keep an eye on the closet door. You see it open stealth-
ily, and you see the intruder slip out. Perhaps he'll exit without
her even knowing he has been there, without doing what he
came to do. Despite your relief from suspense, you're a trifle
disappointed.) But Marilyn doesn't drink the glass of milk in
the kitchen. She carries it with her. She'll drink it after she
gets into bed. (*If* she ever gets into bed.) Hearing her foot-
steps, the intruder pops back into the closet. (And you're back
in that delicious agony again.)

The concealed and the revealed

We could go on stretching out the suspense just as long as
your nerves will stand it. Every time Marilyn approaches the
closet, you expect the intruder to jump out at her. You plead
with her to stay away from danger. Before the writer is through
with you, you don't care what happens, so long as the suspense
is relaxed. That's the Known!

Obviously there doesn't always have to be a man in the bedroom closet, but there had better be something in the closet
besides clothes, even Paris models. You will arouse more suspense if you will show early in your story what is there than
if you keep it hidden, unknown, and let it jump out at the
reader. To paraphrase E. M. Forster, if you have only suspense, you don't have a very good story; but if you don't have
suspense, you don't have a story at all. Suspense, to me, is
synonymous with plot. It isn't the unique province of the "suspense writer." All writers must live in that country.

Take, for example, that "practically perfect novel," *The
Light in the Piazza,* by Elizabeth Spencer. (The quotation is
from *The New Yorker.*) Where would the suspense have been
if we had been kept ignorant, until after the wedding, of the
pertinent fact that the bride because of a tragic accident had
only the mind of a ten-year-old? But no one would dream of
concealing that information, you say? Well, just for an experi-

ment, get out some of your rejects and reread them. You may be surprised. Are you sure you have always allowed the reader to see the man hide in the closet? It is unbelievable how difficult it is sometimes to get a student writer (or any writer at times) to say what his story is about—to say it clearly, and openly, and as early in the story as possible; for the short story that means on the first page, in the first paragraph, in the first sentence.

Not "what" happens, but "how"

If suspense lies in the known, another truth emerges: the reader's interest then must lie not in what is going to happen, but how it is going to happen. I have no mind for figures, so I won't hazard a guess as to how many basic plots the experts say there are; but I do remember that they say there aren't many. I'd go further. I'd say that there is only one. When people use "formula" in the pejorative sense, they are speaking out of prejudice. Take any great love story, *Tristan and Isolde, Anna Karenina,* or the latest movie (good or bad). The formula is the known one: boy meets girl, boy falls for girl, boy fears he is going to lose girl, boy finally wins her, and they live happily ever after *or* he does lose her. If you substitute for the word "girl," job or fame, or "quest" for treasure or truth or life, I believe you will just about have taken care of all the story plots in literature.

The important step is that third one: boy fears he is going to lose. Here is the conflict. This is where the suspense lies. In other words, stories are about people, and people are interesting only when they are in trouble, or in conflict. (And that is a reflection that can stop us for a long echoing moment.) Classically there are three basic kinds of conflict: man against man, man against nature or conditions, man against himself. The important thing here is that the fighters must be evenly matched. No fight is any better than its principals. A thrown fight has no interest at all; neither has one that is too heavily weighted for or against one or the other combatant. We will feel sympathy for the underdog, but we have no interest in the fight; we just want it to be over.

It is the same in a story. Do your hero the courtesy of providing him with a worthy opponent, be it another man, the elements, or fate, or himself. In every good story (of whatever genre), there comes a place where the action hangs in balance, where the story can go in either direction, where the outcome is in question. This is the third step of the formula: boy (but let him be a man) fears he is going to lose. Will he or won't he? To be or not to be? Whether he is Shakespeare or the author of a thriller, the writer must make the reader question, worry. If the reader worries, if he identifies with the protagonist's fears, he will read on until he finds out what happens. So, prolong the suspense; stretch it out as far as you can, but—don't let it break.

The importance of timing

We speak of "timing" often in regard to performers. Timing is just as important for the writer as it is for the actor. Perhaps this goes back to the time when the storyteller narrated his stories by mouth, not typewriter, when he was an actor. You must play a scene for all it is worth, you must build the suspense as high as it will go, but you must not try to take it one step higher than the reader will go with you.

Put it another way. Remember the old story about the ghosts? If one ghost is scary, two ghosts will be twice as scary —but ten ghosts won't be scary at all; they'll be humorous, or ludicrous, or boring; they'll destroy the illusion and catapult the reader back into real life. Say that you have our interest because of your heroine's plight. Her husband, the heel, has deserted her with a small infant to care for. Suspense: Is she going to be able to keep the child or not? You can build the suspense by revealing that she has been accused of being unfit to raise a child; perhaps she is in a dubious profession. You might build the suspense further by making her physical condition precarious. She has never fully recovered from the difficult childbirth. *But* don't lay her low with cancer, or anything else truly critical, because, though this could happen in real life and we would give her our sympathy, in fiction our suspense will collapse. We know then for sure that she is not going to manage to keep the child.

A good story always has a man in the closet. In the entertainment story, it is enough to see the intruder hide in the closet and to wait with mounting suspense for the moment when he jumps out. In stories of more lasting value, the writer must make it clear why the man is in the closet, and the better the reason, the better the story.

The essence of tragedy is inevitability—when an irresistible force meets an immovable object (*Romeo and Juliet*). The essence of comedy is not so different. It is the breaking of the mold, but it is inevitable also. Take the clown in the circus: We know he can't ride the horse bareback, or walk the high wire. As soon as he gets up there, we know he is going to fall, and we wait for him to fall so that we can laugh. The wait during which he almost falls but doesn't quite is the period of suspense that makes the fall funnier.

The reader must be told in the very first paragraph what must happen; then it is the writer's task to keep him hoping against hope to the very last paragraph that it won't happen. This is the story that we'd all like to write.

4

PLOT AND LIFE IN
THE POLICE PROCEDURAL

by *Rex Burns*

A MAJOR difference between journalism and fiction is the need for plot: journalism, like the life it reports, does not have plot; fiction can not do without it. This distinction is often masked in the police procedural because the aim of this sub-genre is to be as lifelike as possible—that is, to give the reader the feeling of an actual newspaper story or a factual report of a crime and its solution. Nevertheless, the police procedural, like all fiction, needs unity—the sense of a beginning, a middle, and an end—and I try to give this quality to the kinds of detective stories I write.

First, a few words about the struggle for plot, then some of the ways to hide that struggle from the reader.

If "story" is what happens, "plot" is why it happens; and both the *what* and the *why* come at several levels in the tale. In the past, these have been called the main plot and the sub-plots, and the terms are still good enough to work with. In most whodunits, the main plot is seldom fully revealed until the story's end; that is, the why of a key fact, such as murder, translates as "motive," and when the detective learns that, he has a good line on the villain. Thus, when an unexpected complication occurs in explaining why, our detective bites his pipestem a bit more firmly and mutters, "Aha, the plot thickens." In some of the traditional closed-room puzzles, everybody from the parish priest to the assistant stableboy turns out to have a motive, and the why translates into "means"—usually quite devious—and "opportunity," which the detective must discover before the concluding scene, wherein he aims a loaded finger at the guilty rascal.

In a traditional whodunit, the why is often motive supported closely by means and opportunity; but in real life and in the police procedural that pretends to depict that life, the means tends to be gruesomely evident from the first: gun, blunt instrument, automobile, knife, bomb, fire—all the jolly ways we have of settling disputes conclusively. The why of this type of detective story is often motive alone, or motive combined with opportunity. With motive alone, the greatest part of the story becomes a reconstruction of the victim's life in order to winnow out likely suspects. This was the central plot line I used in *Speak for the Dead,* my detective Gabe Wager's third adventure. When motive tends to be known or soon revealed, the greatest part of the tale focuses on discovering the opportunity to commit the crime. In the police procedural, the search for opportunity is, in fact, a search for evidence to prove legally a known suspect's presence at the scene of the crime. This offers an excellent chance for an author to make use of his knowledge of the technical and scientific side of criminology.

The how-to-prove-it mystery

Unlike the whodunit, the how-to-prove-it tends to reveal early on the crime and the criminal. As a result, the main plot is less dominant, and the structure of the story becomes the chase. This kind of tale requires the writer to sacrifice one of his strongest lures for the reader—revelation of the criminal— and to substitute other interest-building devices: the mood achieved by tone and setting, the personal reflections of the detective, the greater use of sub-plots, the demonstration of police techniques and technology. In the first two Gabe Wager novels—*The Alvarez Journal* and *The Farnsworth Score*—I put the bad guys' names in the titles: no puzzle there. What-long-term suspense exists is in the struggle to locate legally admissible evidence and then to tie it to Alvarez or Farnsworth, and finally to convict them. It's not an easy job, but one, I'm convinced, that is far more characteristic of actual police work than the traditional whodunit. What it demands from the writer is a balancing act between maintaining suspense or interest and making that suspense believable.

One device I've used to sustain reader interest is a thematic one: the law as a hindrance to justice, that is, evidence not legally admissible cannot be used, no matter how damning it is. The absurdities of legal sense versus common sense are as old as the legal profession itself, but it was an issue of particular sensitivity to the street policeman during the decade or so following the Miranda decision.

A word of caution: don't preach. Sermonizing belongs in articles like this one. In suspense fiction, the thematic statements should be dramatized through incident, setting, imagery, brief comments by the characters. Few readers of fiction who pick up a detective story are interested in a philosophical treatise by the author. However, readers can become interested in what a character thinks and feels, provided those things contribute to rather than usurp the action.

Nonetheless, thematic interest cannot offer a complete substitution for suspense in a detective story. At best, this technique will attract readers who are entertained as much by irony as by action; at worst, it will serve to keep only the author interested in what happens next.

In both the whodunit and the how-to-prove-it, the need for drama is constant. One might think of two, or perhaps three, principal high points in the central plot of most stories: the discovery of the victim, the identification of the culprit, and, often, the chase to capture that culprit. That leaves a lot of space to be filled in, and thematic interest seldom does the job by itself. One way to keep the string taut while spinning the yarn is to make use of sub-plots. These might range from a relationship between the protagonist and some other character, to a second or third criminal case somehow related to the main plot. The detective's wife or girl friend, his partners, his informants and bosses—all these create the environment through which the detective moves, and his relationship with them should provide interest at these points where the main plot weakens. Some authors, such as Ed McBain and Dell Shannon, provide a number of criminal activities that take turns on center stage, as the main plot moves in and out of focus. The best novels—police or other—are those that best orchestrate plots, sub-plots, and themes into some kind of pattern.

Craftsmanship

All of these techniques are supposed to heighten the reader's interest, but they won't work if the writing is bad. Characterization, sentence structure, economy, setting, diction, etc.—the demands of craftsmanship are as stringent for good suspense writing as for any other kind of storytelling. But the police procedural, being a "realistic" mode, must also avoid appearing too pat. The bare structure of any story can be hidden—often dictated—by the development of lifelike characters. Pertinent to the successful police procedural is accurate factual and technical information to mask the artificiality of a story's structure. How do those of us who want to write convincing police novels but lack experience in police procedure achieve technical accuracy? The most direct source of information is the local police department, the department of public safety, the sheriff's office, constabulary, posse, what have you. Many local or state police departments have citizen participation programs or public information officers who are usually pleased to cooperate when someone shows interest in their work. My favorite preparation for writing a new Gabe Wager yarn is to share a tour of duty with the detectives of the Denver Police Department as part of their ride-along program. In Denver, the program is open to all citizens, with permission of the Division Chief; and I've never failed to find the officers both courteous and informative. In addition, the D.P.D., like most medium and large-sized departments, has regular public tours of the police facilities from drunk-tank to courtroom, with interesting stops at such places as communications or the polygraph section. Some areas, particularly laboratories, are off limits, but even most of these can be seen by special arrangement.

I find these tours and visits to be particularly useful for establishing the setting and tone of the story. The plot, as mentioned above, has its own literary demands for pattern and unity. This demand is artificial when compared to the chaos and coincidence of life. But the precise detail for a setting—the institutional odor of a freshly waxed hallway, the dents and scratches on an empty waiting-room bench, the distant and unseen jingle of keys—these details can create the necessary illusion of life so important to sustaining reader interest and to fleshing out the bones of the plot. The only way to get that is to go, see, and record.

Technical jargon and street slang

The same caveat applies to language. While the technical jargon of police work tends to remain relatively unchanging, the street slang of station house and patrol car changes rapidly. But language is character, and a writer must develop his ear for the precise phrase, the cadence, the metaphor that helps define character. Only occasionally can the words be used almost verbatim.

Here is a passage from my notes of an interview that took place while I was on night tour with detectives from Homicide Division. A witness, after some cajoling from the investigating officer, said that he'd come to Denver to enroll in one of the community colleges, and that he just happened to be visiting the victim when a third party shot him.

> *Witness:* Sounded like a .22 but it looked like it was on a .38 frame. Chrome plated. I was running so fast I missed this phone booth and ended up at Reese's. There's usually a cop there.
> *Officer:* Did you know what was going to happen?
> *Witness:* Don't know. Don't know. If I'da knew, I wouldn'ta been standing there.
> *Officer:* I want you to tell me slow so I can get it. Or do you want to write it yourself?
> *Witness:* Aw, I can do it. I can write it.

In *Angle of Attack,* the passage became, in part:

> "What kind of pistol was it?"
> "It sounded like a twenty-two—you know that little pop they make. But it looked like it was on a thirty-eight frame. Chrome plated."
> "You could see all that but you couldn't see his face?"
> "Yeah—the light was on it. And he held it out like this. And I'll tell you something else—I wasn't studying his face. I was studying that gun!"
> [Wager] handed Ernie a pen and told him to sit in the front seat. "Can you write down everything you told me? Or do you want me to write it for you?"
> "I can write it man—as good as anybody. I'm going to college!"

The original language and event were interesting in themselves and provided the details for imagination to work on. But to give clearer direction to the dialogue and to have the scene contribute not only to the life of the novel but also to the movement of the plot, a little compression and heightening was required. The trick is to mold the raw material without pressing the life out of it.

Source material

Another way to get the feel of police and criminal activity and language is to read newspapers avidly. Newspaper columns and straight news stories are sources for a wide range of material. I especially like photographs that show details of crimes that have been committed, since that is the closest thing to witnessing them myself. Reporters who have a demonstrated ability to capture colorful speech offer the closest thing to using my own ears. In this respect, Jimmy Breslin is one of my favorites.

Other kinds of reading are also essential. One tour of police headquarters doesn't make the writer an expert, so it's a good idea to have some basic reference books on your shelf. An indispensable aid for me is the *Crime Scene Search and Physical Evidence Handbook,* put out by the Department of Justice and available through the U.S. Government Printing Office. Government Documents provides a wide range of such texts, all of which can be found in the "Subject Bibliographies." A few of the more specialized titles which the crime writer might enjoy are: *Forcible Rape, Medical and Legal Information, Anatomy of a Scam: A Case Study of a Planned Bankruptcy by Organized Crime,* and *Gambling Technology.* Equally entertaining are various FBI publications, also from the G.P.O., such as "Handbook of Forensic Science" and "Flight Characteristics of Human Blood and Stain Patterns." *Crime Investigation,* by Kirk and Thornton (John Wiley & Sons), is used in police training classes all over the country, and though it can be a bit dated in areas of latest technological advances, it is a good basic reference book for the crime writer as well as the crime fighter.

5

PLOTTINGS

by *Max Byrd*

IN TRYING to explain to a correspondent why he wrote so slowly—and with such stubborn, teeth-gnashing difficulty—Raymond Chandler came up with an answer most aspiring writers can understand:

> . . . it was always a plot difficulty that held me up. I simply would not plot far enough ahead. I'd write something I liked and then I would have a hell of a time making it fit in to the structure. This resulted in some rather startling oddities of construction, about which I care nothing, being fundamentally rather uninterested in plot.*

The irony, of course, is that Chandler chose to write detective novels, the most plot-dependent of all narratives. And like every other detective writer, hard-boiled or classic, he had to wrestle with the fact that the detective story is *self-conscious* about plot. It calls attention to its own plot. At its conclusion, the mystery story must not only announce a solution, but must also review its whole earlier narrative in order to call attention to its plausibility and logic. Anyone who sat through the Agatha Christie movie *Evil Under the Sun* will have recognized in Hercule Poirot's interminable reconstruction of the murder the classic device of summary and review that every mystery requires. And anyone who tries to devise a mystery

*Raymond Chandler, *Selected Letters,* Frank MacShane, Editor (Columbia University Press, N.Y., 1981), p. 81

plot will sympathize with Chandler's dilemma: In order to have the story come out right, you simply have to plot far ahead—you have to plot all the way to the end.

My first two Mike Haller mysteries (*California Thriller* and *Fly Away, Jill*) were written according to the trial-and-error procedure that Chandler describes. But when Bantam asked me to write a third Mike Haller novel, they gave me only a year to complete the typescript. Since I would be teaching a full academic schedule throughout that year, the necessity for plotting far enough ahead became urgent: I had not time in the schedule for trial and error or for massive rewritings.

First, I eliminated the stop-and-start process I had been using. I already had my case of detective characters—Haller, his partner, Fred, his friend Dinah—but I had no actual plot beyond the quite shadowy notion that I wondered what would happen if the clichéd threat actually came true: What would happen if Haller actually lost his license to be a detective?

After a solid week of staring at blank sheets of paper, I realized that I was not going to dream up a plot in a vacuum, certainly not a plot that would allow me to write quickly. The steps that I took next were helpful to me; perhaps other detective writers will also find something useful in them.

Plot categories

My first step was to make a catalogue of major detective plot categories that I recognized. I came up with seven:

1. *The caper*—perhaps the simplest of all plots, but in the right hands always a winner. This plot is basically serial: You know what the goal is—to rob a train (Michael Crichton's *The Great Train Robbery*), to assassinate someone (*The Day of the Jackal*)—and your plot consists chiefly of the preparations your protagonist makes. There is no need for reversals and surprises (until the end), for the plot is almost always a step-by-step account of assembling collaborators, scouting positions, introducing policemen, etc. Much of the enduring appeal of the caper plot comes from the same psychological source *Robinson Crusoe* first tapped: our vicarious

delight in planning and constructing elaborate schemes and struc-
tures.

2. *The ticking clock*—Nobody has done this better than Crichton in
   The Andromeda Strain, but almost every detective writer ap-
   preciates the built-in suspense of a deadline. Many writers have
   found the simple device of giving each chapter a date, place, and
   time of day makes a stubborn plot fall into place.

3. *Get me out of here*—The master of this is Peter O'Donnell, whose
   Modesty Blaise stories always have the same plot: the heroine is
   captured and imprisoned, and the British Cavalry come riding over
   the hill in the nick of time. (Donald Hamilton often uses this category in his Matt Helm novels.)

4. *The puzzle*—Agatha Christie territory. By her own account, she
   used to dream them up while doing the dishes. Perhaps it's because
   I can't think them up, but I agree with Chandler that there's no
   such thing as an honest detective puzzle. (I note in passing that the
   puzzle always stresses plot over character or style and is better
   adapted to comedy than to the realistic novel.)

5. *The Oedipal*—Ross Macdonald has made everyone aware of a fundamental principle of detective plots. There is always an *earlier
   crime.* This plot requires you to treat the present crime as a conse-
   quence of an earlier, perhaps forgotten one, and it requires you to
   push far back into the past to explain the present. A beautiful
   Chandler example, with no "oddities of construction" at all, is *The
   Long Goodbye.*

6. *Renaissance and Reformation*—the Pygmalion theme, in which an
   ordinary protagonist, mysteriously swept into crime or intrigue, is
   transformed into a stronger, harder, more dangerous person; or in
   which the hero remakes another person in his image. This works
   very well in spy and revenge stories such as leCarré's magnificent
   The Little Drummer Girl, where the girl "Charlie" is remade into a
   terrorist, and also in a psychological detective story like Robert
   Parker's *Early Autumn,* where the detective Spenser tutors a boy
   into manhood. Many of Simenon's Maigret detective novels re-
   volve around the related mystery of a character who suddenly
   walks away from one life and takes up a new life and identity in
   another city.

7. *Reflective plots*—I thought of two examples at once: Dick Francis'
   Whip Hand . . . and *King Lear.* Here the subplots and the main
   mystery plot must converge in a resolution. Note that the first-
   person plot (the kind of narrative most beginning mystery writers
   should use, I think) requires that the subplot also concern the
   detective. In a third-person narrative, the subplot can employ different characters to reflect the various themes. To my mind this is
   by far the best of the plot categories because it relies upon the
   profound and commonplace truth that action arises from character.

Spinoffs

When I had studied this list I realized that any major plot category can be used as an element in another plot category. The caper plot can run according to a deadline—the ticking clock—and can, for example, conclude with a Modesty Blaise style escape. Any of the categories can be reduced to episodes or even scenes; and every kind of plot can employ reflecting subplots.

In plotting *Finders Weepers,* my third Mike Haller story, I found myself following three introductory steps that made use of what I had learned. For two weeks, I went back and forth each morning, doing and redoing in no special order one of these three things.

1. I wrote sketches of all my possible characters—biographies of one or two pages in which I described them physically, gave their ages, their schools, their quirks. Most of these had to be repeated several times, growing longer and longer; but when I came to the actual writing the sketches were invaluable and could often be used word-for-word.

2. I made a list of scenes. These were not plots but simply the kinds of things that could happen if Haller lost his license. He would be harassed by the police, for example, he would lose his license to carry a gun and would have to get one covertly (or do without!); in trying to regain his license he would threaten the criminal, who would therefore have to appear in the story at an early point to stop Haller's progress. I also thought of locations where scenes might take place. (Because small quantities of cyanide are often present in a greenhouse, I knew I wanted a scene to take place there. I also thought about chase scenes on boats in San Francisco Bay.) The order of all these scenes was completely random, but the simple presence of the list continually suggested other possibilities and additions.

3. I made a long summary—four or five typed pages—of the story that might develop. This was by far the hardest thing to do. The summary of the end was much thinner than the beginning, but it served as an extremely useful framework in which to start writing. I know some writers who make much longer summaries—fifteen or twenty pages or more—and they find the actual writing almost automatic, though of course every plot changes in some way as soon as you set it in motion.

Visualizing the end

Finally, I worked according to a principle that I had thought out myself, but that I subsequently discovered in John Braine's excellent book *Writing A Novel*. I tried to visualize the last scene in the story first. At its simplest level, after all, plot is no more than a mechanism for change. If you know what the end of your story looks like, you can far more easily picture what the beginning will have to be. But for me—and I think for many other writers—this last scene must be strongly visual. It is not enough to say that Mike Haller must of course regain his license. I had to *imagine,* in the strictest sense, what that scene would look like when it happened. The scene I imagined, in fact—long before title, setting, or even situation—was a fight in the surf, near the Seal Rocks on the edge of San Francisco Bay. I didn't know whom Mike was fighting, or why. But the physical setting was dramatic—I had seen it many times—and a battle in the water somehow suggested to my mind the psychological elements of frustration and release that Haller would have to go through in order to regain his license, that is to say, in order to regain his identity as a detective.

I had in mind another principle as well: the detective story, as I've said, ends by repeating itself. But I have long thought that *all* plots end by repeating themselves. Poirot does not repeat the story of the murder exactly as we saw it, however; he and all other detectives repeat the central episode in a new way. They give the unknown murderer a name, they call attention to a detail, they introduce an unexpected fact or motive. The plot, in other words, must remind us of what it has changed. We have to hear echoes of its beginning before we can understand that it is over. This is as true for *Great Expectations*—in which Dickens' famous second ending shows us Estella at last not rejecting Pip—as it is for *The Big Sleep,* in which Marlowe once again finds himself in Vivian Regan's bedroom sparring with her over the disappearance of Rusty

Regan, but this time telling her (and us) his version of the story with which we began in the famous opening chapters. Chandler may indeed have been uninterested in plot, but no writer, I suspect, can be uninterested in design.

6

IRONY AND SURPRISE

by *Stanley Ellin*

I AM A READER and writer of mystery stories who thinks that the works of Sir Arthur Conan Doyle are a monument to boredom. A pox, I say, on the posturing Holmes and the goggle-eyed Watson. Anathema to The Baker Street Irregulars, that unholy gang of worshipers at the shrine of Sherlock. The next time they drink a toast to him, may their wine turn to sarsaparilla in the glass!

Do I stand alone in this matter? I do not think so. A secret agent (he is allowed to keep ten percent of the information he brings me) recently mentioned other symptoms of revolt in the ranks, but I am not overly optimistic about them. The sad truth is that we anti-Holmesites are a rabbity breed of iconoclast, indeed, and I admit to being as long-eared and cotton-tailed as any. Not long ago, I let fall an unfavorable comment about the Master in the presence of a fellow mystery writer. Before I could say another word I was pierced by a look so terrible that I immediately slunk away to find solace among the potato chips and beer, and was mightily glad that I outweighed the enraged writer by some thirty pounds, or, as Holmes would say, two stone and thruppence. At even weights I was a goner, and knew it.

The trouble is that I discovered Holmes much too late in life. Sir Arthur is, of course, a highly satisfactory writer for the youthful audience which, in its innocence, may readily mistake his cardboard figures for People, his tedious declamations for Dialogue, and his heavy-handed devices for Plotting. But the reader who is introduced to all this for the first time in his middle years will only be distressed by it. This reader is not only likely to be suffering from tired blood and constriction of the income tax; he has also had the chance, over the years, to read some mystery stories written for the adult audience. He will, after his initial plunge into Holmes, come to the surface wondering if someone is not playing a joke on him.

That is what happened to me. At the age of thirty-five— *midway in life's journey,* as Dante, a noted Italian mystery writer, phrased it—I was led by a friend to take the plunge. So keen is my regard for this man that he could have the Hathaway shirt off my back and the patch from my eye merely by crooking a finger at them, but before I was halfway through his Collected Works of Doyle I knew that even a friendship like ours had its limits. I returned his book and explained that he would have to take me Doyle-less, or not at all. We are still friends, I am glad to say, but no thanks to Sherlock Holmes for that.

Now, what is it about the Works which could lead to such a crisis? It is not, strangely enough, those little matters of characterization and style previously referred to, although they were certainly hard to take. But, I must confess, I read Henry James and Theodore Dreiser with pleasure, and there are times when they make Doyle's technique look positively graceful. No, what is lacking in Doyle is something of much greater importance. In a nutshell, his stories are all built on *surprise,* and, at the same time, are totally devoid of *irony.*

Surprises with significance

There is a vast distinction between surprise and irony. When you read *Gulliver's Travels* as a child (in a nicely expurgated edition, I trust), you read it for surprise, and through Swift's inventive genius you were provided with that on one page after another. When you reread the book as an adult, you read it for irony, and Swift's merciless opinions of 18th-century mankind provided that in full measure. You may gather from this that the difference between surprise and irony is akin to the difference between child and adult, and so it is. Or, in terms of the classic mystery story, it is the difference between Sir Arthur Conan Doyle and Edgar Allan Poe.

Doyle wrote a massive collection of short mystery stories, and there is not a glimmer of irony in them. Poe wrote four little mystery stories—the four from which the entire *genre* flowered—and they are replete with an irony that invests them with true literary worth. That is not to say that the reader can be counted on to consciously seek out or find the irony underlying a piece of fiction. But if it is there he will somehow sense it, and he will know that he is seeing something more than a man pulling rabbits out of a hat.

When you have the chance, reread Poe's "Murders in the Rue Morgue" and "The Purloined Letter." The first implies very sharply that when an ape batters a woman to death he is acting remarkably like a man. The second makes note of a universal human characteristic: when a human being searches for a lost object, the last place he will look for it is right under his nose. These are dramatic ironies. These are the elements which, underlying the factor of surprise that the mystery writer must weave into his story, give that surprise its deepest significance.

I am afraid that most of those writers who are bending their efforts to the mystery story for the first time are not aware of this. Or, if aware, are concealing the awareness stoically. They are so intrigued by the horrific nature of crime itself, and by all the appurtenances which can be crowded into a story about a crime, that they approach their maiden efforts in somewhat the spirit of a boy getting to work on his first Erector set. The difference in the long run is that while the boy knows his bridge isn't a real bridge, the hopeful writer doesn't know that his story isn't a real story. It *looks* like a real story, doesn't it? It has everything in it that a mystery is supposed to have, doesn't it? Then why does it keep bouncing back in the mails like something attached to a rubber band?

What makes a **real** mystery story?

My answer is intended only for those who have a lively imagination, an ability to create plausible characters, a sound plotting sense, a command of the English language, and a typewriter.

First, what *is* a mystery story? And I mean by that, how would you define the term "mystery story" in the present-day sense? Do not rush to answer that; there are pitfalls ahead. The wise course is to get an armful of various mystery magazines—with emphasis on *Ellery Queen's Mystery Magazine* and *Alfred Hitchcock's Mystery Magazine*—and to spend a few weeks of time reading them. Ready now? All right, put down your definition and compare it with this one:

A mystery story is a short prose fiction that is, in some way, concerned with a crime.

That's all there is to it. It's as vague and all-inclusive and generally infuriating as that. And if your definition departs far from the above, if it glitters with fine-sounding technicalities and criminous terminology, you will please write on the blackboard one thousand times: *I was completely out of touch with what mystery magazine editors wanted.*

The fact is that your story can be one thousand words long, or ten thousand. It can have a detective, a victim, clues, and deduction, or none of them. It can have a mystery, secret or not, just as you choose. It can be savage or tender, mocking or serious, coarse or delicate. It can, in brief, be anything you want to make of it, as long as it has some concern with a crime.

To the writer who has been becalmed in the horse latitudes of rejection slips, this information sometimes comes as an unpleasant shock. At least, while he was becalmed he knew where he was. Now he has the feeling that his otherwise snug—albeit unprofitable—craft has slipped her moorings and is drifting off into a fog. Especially is this true of the writer who has been grinding out variations on the ancient Dead victim-Omniscient detective-Clever clues theme. The one which ends up with: "You, Jenkins, are the killer, and here, madame, are your jewels."

But once the initial shock passes he will find that he is drifting, not in a fog, but on wide, inviting seas. There is virtually no limitation on what he may use as story material, or on how he may organize it. A writer is at his most confident and capable when he deals with things familiar to him. Now our mystery writer is free to discard the brilliant police detective and the tough private eye, who were remote and unlikely acquaintances of his at best, and turn to the people next door, the people in the office, the people in his home. They may not be the exact material around which a given story should be constructed, but they will serve as guides to the people and ideas which will finally kindle genuine inspiration.

We have now come full cycle back to the matter of irony. Dramatic irony, that is. In a way, the names of Ellery Queen and Alfred Hitchcock should have indicated the inevitability of that, because to the informed their names are synonymous with that word "irony." Give them a story which in some way invokes the ancient spirit of Hubris—the ironic self-destruction inherent in the act of flouting the gods—and they are the happiest of men. They like surprise, but they will buy irony.

Dramatic impact

If finding a proper definition for the modern mystery story was difficult, finding a proper definition for dramatic irony is a hundred times more difficult. Anyone asked to do it in so many words will soon find himself in the position of the man asked to define a corkscrew. The hands then draw spirals in the air, examples and comparisons flood the mind, but the exact, neat definition remains elusive. It is best to go directly to the examples themselves.

One such example is provided by the story of a lynching. The classical formula would suggest that we have a victim killed by a lynch mob, whereupon a wise and sternly just sheriff manages, through courage and clever deduction, to apprehend the leader of the mob. A pretty good story could be written around this framework, and a few have been.

But the finest story written about a lynching—the lynching of a Negro in the Deep South in this case—is by John Steinbeck. He was not interested in the brute scene itself, in the mob, in justice being done. He was interested only in one of the men who attended the affair, and who, very probably, did not even take physical part in it. And the entire story is about the small episode wherein this man returns to his home and is greeted there by his wife who does not know where he has been. Then she takes one look at him, and flies into a fury. He has just been to bed with another woman, she rages, and she knows that—because of the expression on his face!

Another example is provided by Somerset Maugham's "Miss Thompson," the short story later dramatized under the title, *Rain*. It is too familiar to warrant outlining here, but suffice it to say that its naked revelation of Reverend Davidson's true character at the end is a classical example of tragic irony.

And, finally, we have one of the greatest short stories ever written, "The Procurator of Judea" by Anatole France. Two old friends meet, after years of separation, at the baths in ancient Rome. The story is simply their dialogue during the few minutes of their meeting. Old politicians both, they reminisce about political affairs long dead and forgotten. One of the men is named Pontius Pilate, and he is full of pleasant recollections of his younger and heartier days. Slowly, the talk turns to the time when he was administrator of the outlandish province of Judea, and slowly, as we know it must, it moves toward a reference to the Christ. It is the friend who makes the reference, and he waits while Pilate muses over it.

"Jesus?" Pilate murmurs at last. "Jesus—of Nazareth? I cannot call him to mind."

That is the final line of the story, and you can read that story, and reread it again and again, and still get the same terrible impact from that line. It is not surprise which gives it to you, because once you know any story it can have no further surprise to offer. But it is irony—the peak of tragic irony— which is the deep, abiding chord under the small note of surprise.

If any of the three stories used as examples here arrived in manuscript, unknown and by an unknown writer, at the offices of *Ellery Queen's Mystery Magazine* or *Alfred Hitchcock's Mystery Magazine,* they would be bought on the spot. Almost no other magazine editors—and, irony of ironies, I include those who originally published them—would today give these tales the eager reception which the best mystery magazine editors would.

Does this mean that the writer who cannot hope to equal Steinbeck or Maugham or France at his best must, perforce, give up the idea of writing mystery stories altogether? Obviously, it does not. If it did, we would all be out of business tomorrow, perish the thought. But it does mean that the neophyte must stop right here and take careful stock.

No editor will buy pale carbon copies of wearily familiar stories—the routine stories which are accepted by the heedless as synonymous with mystery writing. On the other hand, no editor really expects to find another "The Procurator of Judea" in his slush pile tomorrow. What he would like to find there, however, are stories which try to achieve the impact and irony of that masterpiece, no matter how far below it they may fall. He knows that the writers of such stories are his writers of tomorrow.

7 METHOD FOR MURDER
by *Loren D. Estleman*

OF ALL FICTION, the detective story has tended most often to reflect the sophistication of its readers. This explains why a mainstream classic like Joseph Conrad's *Lord Jim* remains as fresh today as when it appeared in 1900, while the first Ellery Queen adventure, *The Roman Hat Mystery,* published nearly thirty years later, is all but unreadable.

The distinction has little to do with quality, as some of the western world's finest writers spent their careers breaking down alibis and tracing buttons clenched in victims' fists. Rather, constant exposure to the mystery form, whether directly or by osmosis, has taught the average reader most of the tricks of diversion that were daring and new in Queen's time but rob the story of its mystery in this more worldly era.

Thinking like your detective

Increasingly, the detective-story writer has to come to rely upon story value over gimmickry in his incessant attempt to hold his audience. Just as life itself has grown more complicated with time, so must the plot of the mystery, and with it the need to occupy the reader with a story intriguing enough on its own to keep his attention through its many detours and 180-degree turns. And in order for the writer himself not to become lost, he will do well to think like his detective.

I'm often asked if the Machiavellian nature of my mysteries

requires a more detailed outline than the average fictional plot. It surprises people to learn that I never outline and seldom know where my story is going when I start writing. As a result, I often find myself desperately treading water during the writing process to avoid drowning in the high tide of unresolved situations, implausible coincidences, and inadequate motivations. When this happens, I simply take a deep breath and throw my arms around my detective, trusting him to lead us both to shore. Once I ask myself how Detroit private eye Amos Walker would react to this or that development, I'm as good as rescued.

Example: Two-thirds of the way through *The Glass Highway,* my fourth Amos Walker mystery, I came to a shrieking halt when all of Walker's leads dried up and it appeared that he and I would never learn what became of the mystery woman for whom he's searching. Like a detective, I went back over the facts, flipping through the early manuscript pages until I found this soliloquy of Walker's, delivered to that same woman:

> ". . . The city prosecutor runs the town, and he's a crook. The police department has several hundred thousand federal revenue-sharing dollars tied up in enough electronic flash to remake *Star Wars,* but what the cops get the most use out of is their twelve-volt cattle prods. Any Saturday night you can ring three longs and two shorts on some rich resident's doorbell and be shown into the basement where a dogfight is going on. There's a former city attorney named Stillson on the main drag who specializes in probate work, but if you're a friend of a friend and have twenty thousand to spare he'll make you the proud parent of a brand-new black-market baby. If you're hot, he'll sell you a complete new set of identification for a grand. . . ."

As originally drafted, the speech was intended only to provide color on a corrupt suburban community and help delineate Walker's mildly crusading character. But now I realized that he had inadvertently supplied the woman with a means of escape through the information about the attorney who sells false identification papers. When Walker remembered this, it gave him a new handle on the case that eventually led to its solution—and me to a bang-up conclusion for the book.

Call it luck or the subconscious at work, I am continually inserting such carpenter's eyes for no reason that I can fathom other than that they seem to lend more depth to the story, only to come up a hundred pages later with just the hook that will fit into one of them. I should add, however, that I wind up removing a number of those that continue to flap loose from the final draft, something I would probably not have to do if I outlined the project first. The decision whether to blueprint a book beforehand or let it grow naturally is the writer's own and should depend on the amount of control he can bring to a work in progress.

Playing fair with the reader

To sharpen the pivotal point in *The Glass Highway,* I was obliged to go back to that early soliloquy and give the crooked attorney a name, something he didn't have previously, so that the woman could be expected to have made contact with him later. It's necessary to plant such seeds early on to avoid having too many convenient explanations flying out of left field during the inevitable expository sequence at the climax. In mystery parlance, this is called playing fair, giving the reader a chance to solve the puzzle with the facts at hand, but in the larger fictional sense it has to do with plausibility. All the labor you put into making your detective a believable character will come to nothing if you allow him to make a string of brilliant deductions in a short space of time without substantiation. If, as is the ideal, the reader has failed to anticipate your solution, he should be able to look up from the page and say, "Sure, why didn't I think of that?"

Perversely, this makes the detective-story writer's job more difficult, for now he must insure against making his mystery too transparent. At this point, a follower of the classic English school would drag the well-known red herring—a phony suspect or a false clue—across the path to divert the reader. But because the device is so well known, it is no longer enough. It thus becomes the writer's chore to take it one step further and create an entire new subplot to pull over the thin place, concealing it and drawing attention away from it. This practice is by no means new—Dashiell Hammett invented the whole business of the search for the Maltese Falcon more than fifty years ago expressly to prevent his readers from looking too closely into the murder of Miles Archer—but it's still effective when handled skillfully, and carries the extra advantage of making the story more interesting and realistic. Any police officer will attest to the fact that real-life mysteries are often obscured by such peripheral matters.

There will come a time, too, when your murderer seems too obvious. When this happens, don't panic. Approach the problem head on and have your detective either consider and reject the character as a suspect until more evidence is in, or just number him among the others and let the reader make of the facts what he will. It's O.K. if he suspects the truth. The writer's only obligation is to provide choices. Do not make the mistake of fitting the crime to the least likely suspect, as readers have long since been aware of that chestnut and will automatically consider the "least likely" the culprit.

How many clues

Never underestimate the detective-story fan's capacity for pleasure in correctly identifying the murderer, or for hostility when he fails. One reviewer grumpily accused me of chicanery in *The Midnight Man* for exposing one of its more likable characters as a murderer. But I had set out all the clues fairly; he was just out of sorts because he'd missed them. Still, the tightrope between giving away too much and not giving away enough should be trod carefully. The reader might often be abreast of the detective, sometimes behind, but he must never, never be ahead, or respect is forfeit.

The writer who has avoided making his mystery too easy runs the danger of making it too complex, losing the reader among the red-herring subplots, tangled motives, and enigmatic characters. This is not as disastrous as it could be, as long as he has succeeded in placing story value ahead of whodunit. But some sort of lifeline should be provided to pull the reader to safety. At such times, I like to remember the way Felix the Cat used to stop the action midway through his cartoons, turn toward the viewer, and say something like, "Boy, am I in trouble. The Master Cylinder has me trapped. . . ," thus bringing late arrivals up to date. Without being so blatant, the detective might at this point freshen faulty memories through dialogue or introspection. After a significant development in the plot of *Motor City Blue,* I had Walker light up one of his ubiquitous Winstons and muse:

> The Kramer burn was related to the Shanks killing, which was related somehow to Marla Bernstein's/Martha Burns' disappearance. If Beryl Garnet was telling the truth, her description of the man who bankrolled Marla's room and board in the cathouse on John R fit Freeman Shanks as well as it fit a thousand other guys. That explained the attempt to disguise himself during his visits, which was unnecessary if the old lady never watched television or read a newspaper as she claimed, but he wouldn't have known that. . . .

And so on. It's plausible as well as helpful, since your detective is human and can be expected to have to arrange his impressions from time to time in order to keep them clear in his own mind. The average reader has as much trouble identifying with genius as has the average writer.

Unraveling the plot

Mysteries that fail usually do so in their closing pages. This is the place where, no matter how scrupulously you have planned your surprises, the detective and the other main characters must unravel the more knotty details of the plot through dialogue. This can be tedious at the one point where it's crucial not to be. Some kind of tension is necessary to hold the reader's interest while all this talking and explaining is going on. Someone must be holding a gun or someone must be inching toward a lamp cord. Suspense must be maintained. This expository scene from *Angel Eyes* speaks for itself:

> "Find that gun," he told the towhead, jerking his chin in the direction of the Cadillac.
>
> Tim grumbled something about just having gotten his suit back from the cleaners, holstered his .45, and got down on his hands and knees to peer under the car. I moved back a step.
>
> "He had a stroke." Clendenan was watching the tableau in the doorway. "Not five minutes after he burst in looking for Mother. He collapsed, and when he finally came to, it was obvious that his brain was affected. Sometimes he's lucid. The rest of the time he's like a ten-year-old. . . ."
>
> "It isn't under there." Tim climbed to his feet and dusted off the knees of his trousers.
>
> "Look on the other side," said the secretary.
>
> While he was watching the bodyguard circle the car I slipped the revolver into the side pocket of my jacket and left it there with my hand around it. . . .

By switching its emphasis back and forth between competing acts as in a two-ring circus, the scene builds anticipation while imparting necessary data. Without the promise of some kind of fireworks at the end, the unfolding of the mystery can be about as riveting as a monotonic reading of the Dead Sea Scrolls.

As the detective story continues evolving to meet the ever-shifting interests of a developing culture, the rules governing its structure must change as well. But the writer who wishes to reach his public cannot go wrong by remembering that he is telling a story first and creating a mystery second. By placing himself in the role of his detective, planting seeds, juggling subplots, and respecting reality, while catering to his audience's love of challenge, he will solve the always intriguing problem of how to attract readers. Which in the end is really the most important mystery of all.

8

HOW TO DEVISE AN INGENIOUS PLOT

by *Rosemary Gatenby*

BECAUSE I write suspense fiction, people often say to me, "You must be very imaginative." I don't think so; if I were, I'd be able to sit down and think up a dandy plot at will. Other writers may well do that, but for me it's a matter of waiting till a suitable idea comes along. I don't do Gothics, or procedurals, or private-eye books, or any kind of series, so sometimes it's quite a wait.

My decision to settle on mysteries was the result of an unscheduled and lonely stay in a hospital in a strange city, years ago. It was a stack of Agatha Christies that got me through the ordeal. The cozy fireside teas; clandestine chats in the garden; visits with old friends; impending dangers; shocking murders; tantalizing puzzles . . . I don't know what I would have done without all these for company. I decided that writing mysteries was not mere frivolity—they were needed. And so I set to work.

I haven't yet gotten to writing about cozy fireside teas; I have felt quite at home with mysteries and love doing them. Since I started writing, mysteries as a class have changed— mine along with many others of the genre. They have become less the formal puzzles of some years ago; they are concerned more with characters and background in a suspense form. They are closer to being mainstream novels. Bringing me back,

as time goes on, closer to what I wanted to do in the first place
—write for-real novels. With the passage of time I have, in
fact, acquired some measure of those things I lacked when I
started—*some* philosophy of life, *some* ability to cast light on
the relationships between people. These things have been finding their way into my books as I, along with mysteries, have
evolved.

Recognizing a good idea

Usually the subject for a book comes to me without warning—most often from a newspaper story, but sometimes from
an incident I've heard about. I recognize it as a book idea by
the instant feeling of excitement it generates, and by a certain
"inevitability" of the story.

Remember when Howard Hughes disappeared from his
high-security living quarters in Las Vegas, resulting in much
speculation in the press? From this incident sprang my novel
The Season of Danger—which was not about Howard Hughes.
It's largely an action story set in Texas and Mexico, its concern a wealthy, reclusive novelist who's been taken prisoner
by his own guards. It came of my wondering about the possible
risks of living hidden away behind a private security system.

Another book of mine stemmed from some remarks about
an apparent suicide. "She wasn't the kind of person who would
have killed herself," her neighbor told me. "And her husband
behaved so *oddly* . . ." But when I wrote *Hanged for a Sheep*,
the story was the reverse of what I thought the truth might
have been. The husband was the hero, but suspicion of him
caused much of the book's action.

The important thing about a book idea is that it be a good
one—with potential, with momentum. I test mine for the following:

1. It must be something that has not already been done—
that is new to *me*, at least.

2. It must be *interesting*. There must be excitement and an

element of mystery in the events that are to take place, and the protagonist(s) must be of sufficient stature to be worth the reader's attention.

3. The idea must have sufficient potential for ongoing action and a progression of developments.

4. The story must present a challenge to me as a writer.

What to do with a suspense plot

Each author has his own methods, certainly, of working out a plot. Also, the needs of one book will be different from another. However, I can give you several suggestions which usually work for me.

STEP 1. *A double strand.* I start with a double strand—the crime filament and a man-woman situation. Conflict between the sexes makes for more interest, and the possibility of eventual romance is an added element of suspense.

STEP 2. *A story line.* A good idea or situation is one in which the beginning contains the possibility of a fascinating ending. This is what I meant by a certain "inevitability." So when you begin the story, you already have somewhere to go with it. My story *never* follows or parallels that of the true-life occurrence which set me off on it. Often my characters themselves determine which way things go—which is one reason I don't outline more than the first half of the book before beginning. I do have, however, a general idea of where we are going to end up.

STEP 3. *A double version.* The plotting method that often works best for me is to figure out the story as it first came to me, with the crime, the perpetrator and his motive; then think of someone else who could have done it, and then start over, creating a second string of relationships and happenings for this person in his new role. The second version thickens the plot, gives more material with which to work.

In *Deadly Relations,* for example, I wrote of a politician whose wife stands in the way of his ambitions. Until almost the end, the crimes all seem to belong to this man. Not so. The one responsible is the woman Bruce once loved, who tries to further his career in the belief that she will get him back from his wife. The politician turns out to have been mostly a victim. Bruce was my *original* villain, Iris the second version.

STEP 4. *Red herrings.* Red herrings seem to appear spontaneously, from the tendency of subsidiary characters in going about their business to do so in a suspicious-seeming way.

STEP 5. *Deceptions.* From successful deception springs surprise. And surprise is what makes your plot "ingenious."

One way to mislead is to give a fact, or an incident, and immediately have your protagonist make an assumption about it which points in the wrong direction. The pull of the story line should drag the reader along on this mistaken path instead of letting him think for himself. Even if the reader suspects this is the wrong way, he will be uneasy (this, too, is suspense) about the hero's persisting in his misguided course—and will be happy later to have his original guess proved right.

In another means of deception, nothing is presented which isn't true, but much is left out, thus creating a faulty context in which certain things will be read. The reader, knowing nothing of the gaps, is trapped by his own logic into making assumptions that are incorrect. I use this technique when I have placed the reader in the mind of a character who's guilty of something. For instance, Dwight, in *The Season of Danger,* worries about the hazardous mission Jack has undertaken. The reader assumes he's worried about his friend Jack—but later will look back and realize that Dwight was worried for fear his own part in the conspiracy would be discovered. Much is *trompe l'oeil* in a suspense book; the reader is tricked into seeing something different from the actuality.

I sometimes use "magic tricks" to delude readers. A basic

technique of magicians is to keep the audience so busy watching some inconsequential bit of action that they miss the important part of the trick. I tried this in *Evil Is As Evil Does.* The security of the bigamous "heroine," who walked away from her first marriage when she survived a train wreck, is threatened by a man who was on the train. The reader is kept so busy watching Betty squirm for fear Harry will give her away that Harry's actual role in the story goes unnoticed until late. *He* has more to hide than *she* does, because he murdered his father-in-law during the wreck—as Betty at last deduces. (And only she knows he was on the train.)

This method achieves its effect by emphasis—by presenting important facts as if they were only background details instead of key plot pieces, and by keeping attention riveted on what *seems* to be the main action.

Another magic trick is one done with time. In *Hanged for a Sheep,* my murderer, Joel Davis, was above suspicion: how could he have killed Enid Weir when he'd never heard of the woman until after her death? He supposedly hears of her only *because of* her death, which triggers the revelation by Joel's wife of her own long-hidden secret, an illegitimate child. Twelve years before, Jeanette had given the baby to her cousin Gil and his wife Enid, who lived in another town. Now, with the foster mother dead, Jeanette hopes to get her child back; at last she finds the courage to tell her husband about little Margaret. The reader watches—the dramatic interest centered on how Joel will take this news about his wife's past. There is a long scene, and then:

> He had put his hand over his eyes, as though shielding them from some harsh light. "Why didn't you tell me?"

And so it is established that he has never been told, and therefore knew nothing about the baby or its foster mother, Enid Weir. The reader is sure he knows the facts, because seeing is believing; what you see, surely, is more reliable than what is told you, which after all might be a lie. The truth behind the scene above is that Joel had known all along about the baby and about Enid Weir; his father had had Joel's fiancée investigated before their marriage.

It is essential, when misleading the reader, to be convincing. To this end, it is sometimes wise to use forestalling tactics. If you fear a piece of deception will not pass muster, have your protagonist suspect it and seemingly dispose of possible doubts. Or if you think the reader may guess in any case, tell him as much of the truth as you have to, and lead him down the nearest garden path as to what the relevance of this truth is.

STEP 6. *Difficulties.* The most devious plot twists can be spawned out of desperation—the desperation resulting from your story's hitting a snag. *Deadly Relations* would not work out the way I planned it. It's a boy-gets-girl, boy-loses-girl, boy-gets-girl story. Steve meets the politician's wife when she has fled from her failed marriage. They fall in love, but she disappears. He traces her, and then according to my original plan, the two of them were supposed to work together to expose Bruce's corruptness. Trouble was, the action ground to a halt the minute Steve found Marian again, in her old home town. After the love affair, it was anticlimactic for them to settle down together to amateur detective work. And the moral values were all wrong; this pair weren't the kind to carry on adulterously right in her husband's shadow. I almost gave up on the book.

Then from difficulty came inspiration: I would keep the romantic pair apart, and Steve could go on alone with his investigations. I'd always intended to have the attempted murder of Marian at some point—now I knew where to put it. So Steve reads in the paper that she has been killed by a bomb planted in her husband's car. When he tries to look into the matter, he himself is almost killed. The police, when they discover his relationship with Marian, suspect him of killing her.

Next, he receives a mysterious phone call from Marian and believes she is, after all, alive. Now how could that be? Fact is, in order to escape a second time from her husband, Marian had persuaded her hairdresser to take her place—just long enough for her to get away. But long enough for the hairdresser to be killed instead of my heroine.

One thing led to another, with twists and reversals I couldn't have foreseen. I could never have dreamed them up if I hadn't had to think long and hard about how to get my hero out of an impasse—and my heroine out of his embrace.

So from adversity comes complexity. This is true not only for the writer, of course, but also for the writer's hero: make things hard for him and you will have a better story.

STEP 7. *Spliced endings.* The "wrap-up" of a book is the most exciting part to do. I finish writing, and then I cut and splice the final segments much as a film editor must do a movie—trying for the most suspenseful effects.

Put off unveiling the villain as long as you can. As the end nears, subplots can be finished off, red herrings explained, and loose ends tied; but keep the main thrust of the tale going as long as possible.

When the identity of the villain *must* be revealed, either manage to end the book promptly or see to it that the hero or heroine is at this point hopelessly in the killer's clutches. Any remaining filling in of motivation or past events can then be done while the excitement is still going on. Though *not* by means of a long explanation from the villain while he holds poor Janet at bay with a gun or cleaver; this method is a cliché, and simply not believable.

I generally use the cliff-hanging technique for the final scenes; cut from the imperiled heroine to the hero, just uncovering the last piece of evidence which has the killer's name on it; back to the *more* imperiled heroine, alone with the villain and with her predicament suddenly worsened; back to the hero who is desperately looking for the heroine in the wrong place and figuring out at last why the villain *has* done all this; and will he ever reach Janet in time . . . ? Although an explanation for everything that has happened must be given or at least suggested, and a resolution of the action must be reached, it works well to leave, perhaps, some component of your plot unresolved. In *The Fugitive Affair,* my villain, though his identity is established beyond reasonable doubt, is not brought to justice because he is untouchable—an irony commensurate with the state of law enforcement today, and thoroughly believable.

Surprising and believable

Surprise and believability are the things most essential to an ingenious plot. Surprise comes from your having effectively concealed the true motives and actions of your evil-doers. Believability comes from carefully laid groundwork—all those little details whose relevance goes undetected until the denouement, when they then must serve to convince the reader of the ending's truth.

The most memorable last page is inevitably the one that projects into the future, leaving your reader with the impression that your characters are not shut up within the book covers he has just closed, but are continuing on with their lives in the setting you have made for them.

9

BREAKING AND ENTERING

by *Sue Grafton*

SEVERAL YEARS ago, a long-suppressed desire to write a detective novel began to work its way into my consciousness. I had long been attracted to the genre, spending many a satisfying evening immersed in the intricate puzzles of fictional homicide. As a detective fiction reader, I was experienced; as a writer, I knew absolutely nothing about private investigation, police procedure, forensics, criminal law, or suspense and mystery techniques. Writing novels had taught me how to create character. Writing film and television scripts had taught me dialogue, but plotting was not my strong suit. As I analyzed my position, I wondered if perhaps I should lie down until the urge to try writing detective fiction disappeared. There I was . . . a big fan of Agatha Christie, Ross Macdonald, Joseph Hansen, Patricia Moyes, Robert B. Parker, Rex Burns, et al. The very idea of competing with such craftsmen scared me half to death. I couldn't think of a better reason to jump in.

Intuitively, I knew that writing detective fiction, like Chinese cooking, would require a lot of advance preparation. I began to do research—the single most important step in the writing of any manuscript. I studied articles on mystery and suspense writing. I consulted various texts on mystery and suspense fiction and added Patricia Highsmith's excellent book, *Plotting and Writing Suspense Fiction* (The Writer, Inc.) to my home library, A fingertip search through *Books In*

Print revealed a number of books about private investigation. To begin with, I read three: *Handbook of Criminal Investigation,* by Maurice Fitzgerald (Arco); *The Investigator,* by James Ackroyd (Frederick Muller Ltd.); and *Technics* (sic) *for the Crime Investigator,* by William Dienstein (Charles C. Thomas). Once I settled on a southern California setting for my projected novel, I acquired *California Criminal Law, California Criminal Procedure,* and *The California Evidence Code.* I did additional reading from a local medical school library on the subjects of forensic pathology and toxicology.

The comfort of the familiar

Having armed myself with a broad range of general knowledge, I sat down to decide what kind of detective novel I wanted to try. In the course of my reading, I had isolated three basic types: the police procedural, in which a homicide detective working for a city or county police department undertakes the solution to a murder case; the "private eye" novel, in which a private investigator or insurance adjuster pursues a suspicious death; and a third category, in which an amateur investigates a murder, tracking down the true culprit to clear his or her own name or to protect the reputation of someone else. I felt no particular affinity for the amateur detective, and since I didn't have the skills or the inside knowledge to tackle a police procedural, I was left with option number two, the licensed private detective. Because I felt more comfortable writing from a woman's point of view, I made my detective female. I chose Santa Barbara as my setting (renaming it Santa Teresa in the book) because I had lived there for six years, and was far enough away at that point to distill my own memories into a fictional California locale. My personal recollections were shored up with street maps, travel guides, picture books of southern California and promotional literature published by a Santa Barbara press. Perhaps unwittingly, I was practicing the first piece of advice that most writers are given anyway! Writing about something you know. The detective genre was new to me and challenge enough in itself. After that, I needed the comfort of the familiar to see me through.

Even before I had fashioned a plot, I wrote an opening to see if I could capture the right tone. I tried first person, self-conscious about the echoes from Raymond Chandler and James M. Cain, convinced that I would never find my own "voice" in the midst of theirs. I wrote about two pages, sounding somehow like a shady character trying to palm off a hot watch. Just to demonstrate, I'll include here the original quote. "My name is Kinsey Millhone. I'm what they call a 'dick,' though the term is somewhat of a misnomer in my case. I'm a woman . . . a female adult. Maybe you know the kind. I'm also a private investigator. I'm 36, married twice, no kids. I'm not very tough, but I'm thorough. . . ." This piece of silliness sat on my desk for a year. At intervals, I would try again, generally in the same hard-boiled mocking Mae West accent. At one point in the writing, still without plot, I had Kinsey Millhone called on the telephone by a man who identified himself as John D-O-U-G-H. I knew that I could never sustain an entire book in this manner. Furthermore, I had no desire to do so. I wanted to write a "real" detective novel, not a *spoof* of one. It's clear to me now that because I felt ill-at-ease with the form, my own discomfort was getting in my way, rather like a telephone line being jammed by static. The interference, in my case, was raw anxiety.

Questions to ask yourself

I turned my attention to the story itself and decided to worry about tone some other time. I began to play "Suppose . . ." and "What if . . .," trying premise after premise with characters designated simply as X and Y. Suppose X wants to murder Y and the scheme misfires so that Z is killed instead. . . . What if Z kills X? T figures out that Z is guilty. T tries to kill Z but

misses, killing Y instead. Two murders. Same M.O. Second
murder is revenge for the first. As I played with ideas, the
notes became less sketchy! High blood pressure medication.
Off on business trip. Violent symptoms . . . nausea, vomiting,
cramps. D.O.A. What assumption would be made? Food
poisoning? What kinds of poison can be traced? What is the
procedure? Urine? Blood tests? How long does it take? The
development of the story progressed as I filled in these blanks.

By bombarding myself with questions over a period of time,
I found that some lines of inquiry were more persistent than
others, some more appealing. A few popped up so often that a
tale began to take shape, the questions becoming statements
instead. "A prominent Santa Teresa divorce attorney dies one
night after taking an allergy capsule laced with oleander. His
wife, accused of the murder, is convicted and serves eight
years in the California Institute for Women, hiring Kinsey
Millhone when she gets out on parole to find the person who
really murdered him." X and Y became characters with real
names and individual identities.

I set up a biographical file for each character that came to
mind, again plying myself with questions, this time pertaining
to personality and motive: What kind of person was Laurence
Fife? Why did so many people hate him? I adopted various
personae, telling the same story from different points of view
until I understood each character's relationship to the book as
a whole. Some characters were invented, and some I fleshed
out from people I knew, borrowing traits and mannerisms until
a character sparked to life independently.

Drawing a plot map

By now, two years had passed, and the story was like a
crossword puzzle with most of the answers filled in. Finally,
with a rough sketch plot laid out and the main characters
defined, I began to construct an outline, detailing scenes as I
felt they should occur. Along with the step outline, I drew up a

"plot map" with the character's lives laid out in chart form, indicating births, deaths, marriages, divorces, affairs.

    1961   Laurence Fife (b. 1934) opens own law firm
    1962   Mrs. N.'s suicide
    1963   Sharon goes to work for Laurence; Charlie Scorsoni joins Laurence's firm
    1964
    1965   Charles S. made a partner in Laurence's firm
    1966
    1967   Gwen's affair
    1968   Gwen and Laurence divorce

Many such events were outside the actual time frame of the novel, but they were facts I needed to know, and the "plot map" allowed me easy visual access to complex character histories. In conjunction with the "plot map," I devised a "sequence of events map" in which I determined the order in which events came to pass. Again, this was helpful in keeping tabs on the narrative which stretched back many years. These incidents happened within months of the murder of Laurence Fife and were directly connected to his death.

1973	June	July
	Nikki out of town; Colin at the beach house	

August	September
Family vacation 8-31 through 9-3; Diane sick; dog killed	

October
Rx filled 10-5; Laurence dies 10-8; Libby calls Scorsoni 10-9, when she hears the news

All of these events were essential to the plot, though the book itself opens eight years later, when Nikki Fife gets out of prison and gets in touch with Kinsey Millhone. As with any other outline, scenes were added, deleted or ignored as the developing story dictated. Not every character would agree to say lines of dialogue I had penned in advance. Not every point worked as planned. Still, the map and charts gave me the tangible evidence I needed that I did know what I was talking about and where I meant to go.

Throughout this stage, I continued to amass work sheets in which I challenged every aspect of the project from the smallest detail to the overall point of view.

As I took myself more seriously, the tone I had been searching for began to come through clearly. I realized that I saw the detective novel as a serious examination of contemporary issues. I started the book again at page one, and oddly enough, the actual opening of *"A" is for Alibi* is not that far from my first glimmerings. The tone by then had been molded and refined. I had found a "voice" that I felt comfortable with—my own.

"My name is Kinsey Millhone. I'm a private investigator licensed by the State of California. I'm thirty-two years old, twice divorced, no kids. The day before yesterday, I killed someone, and the fact weighs heavily on my mind. . . ."

10 WRITING A THRILLER

by *Bill Granger*

I WRITE thrillers. Telling you the tricks of the trade is not difficult. Telling you what makes a good thriller is much harder.

Every craft has its tricks, but knowing the tricks is only the first step toward creating a bit of art—and a bit of art is what all good writing is, even good thrillers.

The thriller offers every possibility in literature. Some thrillers are pure junk, some pure escapism. The two categories are not mutually inclusive—a lot of very good escapist reading comes from very skilled craftsmen who aspire to do exactly what they are doing and no more.

Writing a thriller involves a basic choice: What kind of a thriller are you going to attempt? Obviously, not junk—but will it have a serious intent or be written as pure escapism—or will it have elements of both, like a lot of the work of John D. MacDonald, who blends the whimsical side of terror with his dark and telling observations on mankind (through the mouth of Travis McGee)?

But if you're going to write thrillers, you have to understand the term, which was invented by the British, incidentally. In America, we subdivide the category into "spy novels," "adventure novels," "police procedurals," and "mysteries." All of these types fall under the umbrella term of "thriller," a very large genre.

Some thriller literature was always meant to be serious, dealing with serious themes, establishing fully realized characters involved in problems of the human condition. John le Carré is best known in this area today but he has ancestors like Graham Greene and even Charles Dickens. Yes, Dickens, who was so fascinated by the subject of crime and the underworld and sudden death that he would tour the London underworld at night—always in the safe care of a friendly cop on the beat. His research went into his books; his themes are grand but a lot of elements of his plots are just flat-out elements of the thriller.

For years, Graham Greene was carried in the thriller (or mystery) sections of bookstores in the United States. Then, someone decided that he was really a very serious writer, and his books were put into the "general literature" section. Same thing happened to le Carré. I've seen my books in both places in bookstores.

And take the case of the late Ian Fleming. . . . Reading his James Bond stories now—nearly a quarter-century after he wrote them—they still carry zest and color and a love for intricate detail that swings the reader along pleasant paths for the sheer fun of it. Fleming gives you a roller coaster ride—it starts nowhere and ends nowhere, unlike a train—but what a lot of fun along the way. He meant it that way, too.

Violence or the threat of violence

Here is my definition of the term (others might be better, but at least this will give you a ruler to measure what I'm talking about): A thriller is a piece of writing—usually a novel—whose plot development depends on violence or a threat of violence and whose resolution is held in suspense until the last possible moment.

"Suspense" is a key word here. Lots of non-thrillers have violence as a plot theme but there is no suspense about either the act or resolution of the plot. A good romance novel, for example, may have violence in the plot, but the suspense is centered on the love element, not on the violence itself.

My definition may have holes in it, but using it can give you a start toward understanding the problems of writing a thriller.

The following questions should be resolved by you before you put blank paper into a typewriter to start writing your thriller:

1. What's it about, and what's the "MacGuffin"?

The MacGuffin is the all-purpose central question proposed by the book, which creates most of the book's suspense. A book can be a thriller without a MacGuffin, but it's going to be a lot more salable to the commercial market if you have one.*

Example of a MacGuffin: In my book *Schism,* an old priest comes out of Asia after being lost for twenty years in the jungles. Immediately, the various spy agencies of the world want to shut him up or kill him or find out what secret he has brought out. And all of the agencies are sure he has a secret. The question is why? And the MacGuffin is *what the old priest's secret really is.*

The whole novel is driven forward by this particular MacGuffin. Every act of betrayal, every bit of bloodshed, every scene pushes toward the resolution of the question. A good MacGuffin should be presented as early as possible in the book and pulled back through it like a ball on a rubber band— tantalizing the reader to follow until he catches it.

Resolving what the book is all about can resolve the

*Alfred Hitchcock explains that a "MacGuffin" is the plot device, or gimmick, of his films, such as secret plans, a stolen gem, or documents; they are unimportant in themselves but must be vitally important to the characters. Hitchcock suggests that the term might have originated in Scotland, where two men were on a train. The first asks, "What's that package in the baggage rack?" The other answers, "Oh, that's a MacGuffin." The first one asks, "What's a MacGuffin?" The other man replies, "It's an apparatus for trapping lions in the Scottish Highlands." The first man says, "But there are no lions in the Scottish Highlands." And the other answers, "Well, then, that's no MacGuffin." A MacGuffin is actually nothing at all. *(Encyclopedia of Mystery and Detection)*

MacGuffin. A MacGuffin can be a person, place, or thing. The MacGuffin in *Topkapi* is to get the jewels out of their resting place despite the presence of guards and all kinds of security. The MacGuffin in le Carré's *Tinker, Tailor, Soldier, Spy* obviously is discovering the identity of the Mole within the Circus.

Your particular MacGuffin has to be big enough to carry the weight of the book. For example, if all the spy agencies set in motion all their plants and operations in *Schism,* and it turned out the old priest's secret was that he was once married, the MacGuffin would be so slight that the book would collapse under its own weight.

2. The second question sounds simple: *Where will your thriller be set,* and what do you know about the place? But this is tricky. Thrillers depend on place to carry the exotic fragrance of a book—particularly a spy novel.

It is possible to write about a place and never have seen it. Edgar Rice Burroughs wrote all those marvelous Tarzan adventures without ever visiting Africa. But today's editors and readers want a lot of detail and facts, and they are pretty sharp about spotting inaccuracies in your book's setting.

Have you been to London? Well, how are you going to set a book in that city? You can mention London in your book in passing but don't try to fake knowledge of the city for an entire novel. (City guidebooks, maps, magazine travel articles, newspaper items and features can also help with some details, such as names of streets, routes, walking directions, and the like.)

But, you say, "I live in Podunk, Iowa!" Then write about Podunk, Iowa. "In a thriller?" you ask. Of course, I answer calmly. In *Schism,* I used Clearwater Beach, Florida, for much of the action, because I knew the town and the setting was right for me. But the most terrifying scenes in the book take place in Green Bay, Wisconsin. Green Bay. Think about it.

Stephen King's horror thrillers are generally placed in the Maine landscape where he grew up and still lives—and what would have seemed a more unlikely spot for a thriller than Maine?

Robert B. Parker of Boston has created a best-selling series of critically acclaimed private-eye thrillers, using the city he knows best; Evan Hunter (writing as Ed McBain) has created an internationally successful series of police procedurals in an unnamed city that is really the New York Hunter knows so well.

You have to do research to make a good book. It seems you have to be even more realistic in novels than you have to seem to be in nonfiction. But all the research on spy jargon or about the way spies spy becomes paper-thin when your "sense of place" in the book lets the reader down. "Place" is really the unmentioned major character in most thriller writing, and it has always been so, from the days of Poe and Conan Doyle to the alligator-infested swamps of John D. MacDonald's Florida stories.

3. Finally, *what voice should you use and who is your leading character?*

Voice is hard. Mickey Spillane and MacDonald both use the first-person narrative effectively, but a lot of other authors— even experienced pros—find it too difficult to handle in any sort of fiction, especially in thriller writing.

A lot of potential for suspense is lost by using the first-person narrative. Take spy thrillers—you can dance around from place to place, setting forces against each other at the same time to build suspense when using the more conventional third-person omniscient point of view. The potential for suspense is lost to the writer choosing first person.

If you want to use first person, make sure you have a damned interesting narrator. He (or she) has to be at the center of the action, he or she has to evoke all the suspense, he or she has to carry the search for the MacGuffin almost exclusively. More important, he or she has to be damned likable and that can be a problem—how can he or she be a cold-blooded spy, for instance, and still carry along the narrative line?

Choosing your narrative voice probably depends on the leading character in your thriller. The two decisions become so entangled it is just as well to consider them as one decision.

Conan Doyle uses the first-person narrative of Dr. Watson and thus allows himself the luxury of both first-person and third-person narration. Most of the "private eye" school use first person and try to create interesting series characters as part of their technique—Parker, MacDonald, Spillane in the modern era and Hammett and Chandler earlier.

In the case of my "November Man" series, the leading character dictated my choice of narrative mode. November is not unsympathetic, but he's difficult to use as first-person narrator. He is cold, distant, rarely speaks, is filled with all sorts of primal angers controlled (usually) by his intellect and has an utterly cynical and contemptuous view of the world. He also kills people from time to time. Not the sort you invite to your son's eighth birthday party.

To balance his character—which came first in my mind—I needed the relief of third-person narration.

Whatever comes first—the character who will lead your thriller or your idea of how to tell the story—your character has to be nearly as strong as the MacGuffin in carrying the plot. Some thrillers fail simply because the central character is too improbable in the situation or the plot.

Example: If your main character owns a candy store in central Texas, he or she is unlikely to be involved in the world of espionage. It's not impossible to do the trick, but unlikely. And what if your candy store owner turned out to be a literary success—how could you follow with a second book using him or her?

Out of genre

Other quick points:

Some writers overplot their book. Have an outline, sure, but let it flow—sometimes, in writing, the best characters or

twists of plot come as a matter of sudden inspiration, leading
the thriller in a new direction that is better than the old.

Don't worry too much about learning the "spy business"
before writing spy novels. Spies are merely good researchers
and observant people—exactly what good thriller writers are.
The jargon can be picked up in any of the (seemingly)
thousands of non-fiction books exposing the CIA and KGB
and NSA. A real-life spy once told me that spies actually pick
up most of *their* jargon from spy novels, so feel free to invent
something—it may be real terminology tomorrow.

Don't let events catch up with your MacGuffin before you
sell the manuscript. This can happen. I wrote *The November
Man* about two years before the murder of Lord Mountbatten
in a bombing of his boat off the Irish Coast. The book came
out two weeks before the event and the novel parallels the real
event in many places. What if I were turning in the manuscript
when the real event happened? Spy novels and world events
have a way of getting in each other's way. Stick to a realistic
line . . . but try not to anticipate history *too much.*

The best thrillers struggle "out of genre" (as the editors say)
because of character—the way the people of the book are
drawn, how deep they are, how much readers care for them
. . . even readers who don't normally read the genre. Telling
you about plots, MacGuffins and such is like talking about
basic rules of carpentry. But making a wood cabinet as a piece
of art is something the carpenter can't be taught.

11

THE MAKING OF A SUSPENSE NOVELIST

by *William Hallahan*

ONCE UPON a time, I was on the losing side of a now historic battle between two giant advertising agencies over an enormous automotive account. And suddenly I was a creative director with rows of empty offices and no staff. If you've ever lived in a keyed-up atmosphere, you know how addictive and exhilarating stress can be. When it stops, you're still wound tight as a five-dollar watch, but suddenly there are no deadlines, no challenges. Nothing to do.

I wandered into the empty art department of the agency and saw a pile of magazines, opened one, and found a profile of a successful suspense novelist. When I read it, I thought—as every novice would—I can do that. And I did. And this is how I did it.

I put a piece of paper into a typewriter, wrote, "Chapter One," and stared at it for two hours. That blank piece of paper had my undivided attention.

Chapter One *what?* Obviously, I was going to have to write about something familiar to me. I made a list that I still have. It was very short. (I didn't know much): Automobiles, airlines, tropical fish, crab grass, diapers, mortgage payments, Irish families, and several other subjects that had nothing to do with the art of writing suspense fiction. I knew nothing about spies, secret codes, hoods, Mafia, assassins, contracts or guns, so I started a novel about an advertising copywriter who knows nothing about spies, secret codes, hoods, etc., and who is suddenly confronted with the professionally committed murder of his best friend.

It was indescribably bad. I knew it, but I was learning. The problem is that while I'm a fast learner, I'm also a superstar forgetter. And I faced the almost limitless subject of the craft of fiction writing. How was I going to keep all that in my head, especially when every day I added new galaxies of information?

I hit on an absolute gold mine: I bought a ring binder and wrote FICTION WRITING on the cover. I began reading everything in sight on novel writing—critical studies, biographies of authors as well as novels, good and bad (you can learn a great deal from reading bad writers). As I read, I made notes and still do. If the item is short, I copy it with a pen. If it's long I type it; if it's lengthy I Xerox it. Everything goes into the binder.

The first ring binder has grown over the years to three thick binders. They are sectioned off into such subjects as Plotting, Character, Scene, Narrative Technique, Style, Setting, Mood. I've been keeping these notebooks for ten years, and they've been keeping me in comfortable circumstances. I keep my binders current, adding fresh material to them every week, so they never get dated. What's more important, I read through them frequently for ideas.

When I'm plotting a new novel, I reread the section on plotting. *Voilà*! An instant refresher course on that subject— ten years of reading, writing and study boiled down. I'm always amazed with how much I've put in there—ideas, tips, techniques that would have long been forgotten. When I'm developing characters, I read the section on characterization. In other words, I keep going back to basics.

Plot chart

I devised a plot chart to see how each episode in my novel worked and related to the characters. This has been of tremendous importance, because it forces me to explore the same story from the point of view of every main character in the book. It makes a one-dimensional story multi-dimensional, richer, more suspenseful. If I have six main characters in the story, I could write six different novels from the same set of events—six different points of view, six different assessments, philosophies and attitudes. It opens up infinite possibilities. The same story can be a towering tragedy to one character, a comedy to another. And sometimes I discover that I can make my novel much richer by dropping my lead character and giving the lead to another character.

There are two other specific benefits I get from my chart: good, red-blooded villains and a stronger plot. Since the chart makes me tell the story through the eyes of my villains, I soon come to understand them and their motives better. As a result, they become more believable and even more attractive to the reader. And, by getting inside their skins, I invariably come up with new and exciting episodes that I would not have thought of otherwise.

The chart is easy to make. I lay out the story in blocks, like a checkerboard. Each vertical column is a time frame (Monday, Tuesday, last year, whatever). I assign a horizontal row to each character, who tells his version of the story in sequence, through the time frames. In that way, I can look at any time frame and see exactly what all of the characters are doing at that moment.

When I get the chart blocked out, I sit and stare at it, testing every event, every character, challenging everything. I uncover all kinds of discrepancies, and I always see ways to make the story better, ways to increase the suspense, to eliminate unnecessary characters. I might make eight or ten revised plot charts before I'm satisfied.

While your main character is going around kicking in doors, saving ladies from nefarious villains, your other characters are not standing around script in hand waiting to go on stage. They're doing things—and often they're doing things to your hero behind his back that may be more dramatic than what the hero is doing at that moment.

I also keep a "mug file," pictures of faces that interest me as I turn the pages of various magazines. When I cast the characters for a novel, I leaf through the mug file to find an appropriate face, and it often astonishes me to find how a character comes to life from such photographs.

When I begin to write a novel, I have pinned to the wall over my typewriter a chart of the plot and a row of pictures of the main characters.

Find the idea

Does this sound mechanical to you? It is, I suppose, but I've learned from my ring binders that there is a great deal that is mechanical or fixed in novel writing. For example, the old saws are rigid and inviolable—there are only three basic suspense plots: man against man, man against nature, man against himself. Trite? Yes. But by following that, you can save an enormous amount of wandering-around time, staring at walls. All this isn't a substitute for creativity; otherwise anyone could write a best-selling novel from a mathematical formula. I'm a professional writer with a living to make. I need to get my thousand words a day on paper with a minimum of wasted time and with some assurance that I haven't overlooked something vital.

Rule one is to *find the idea*. I think of hundreds and throw most of them away. The idea is what the reader reads on the dust jacket—what makes him buy or pass by. So when I get what I think is a good idea, I immediately write the dust jacket copy—the blurb—and see how it sounds. No matter how well I plot a book, no matter how well I write it or people it with vivid characters, if the idea's dull, or if it's been done before, the reader will buy someone else's novel. Where do I get ideas? Reading, thinking, talking with people—living. I write them down and save them. *The Trade* concerns a plot by a group of German industrialists to reunite Germany by fomenting revolution in Russia—until one day an American arms dealer appears. An earlier novel (my third), *The Search for Joseph Tully,* is about the pursuit of a man by another man through a series of reincarnations spanning 500 years—*until* one day the pursuer catches up with his quarry. *Catch Me: Kill Me* involves an underground railway that smuggles dissident Jews out of Russia to the United States—*until* one day the wrong man comes through. *Until*—that's another word for putting the fox in the hen coop.

Anticipation

There's one aspect of suspense fiction I want to stress. It took me a long time to learn this—it's called anticipation. If your hero is walking down the street and someone jumps out of a doorway and takes a shot at him, the reader is totally surprised. The episode barely registers on his mind. Surprise is the antithesis of suspense.

To get maximum suspense from that event, you need to prepare the reader. You have to show the gunman taking his position, planning his attack, checking his pistol or whatnot. You have to show the hero, preoccupied, walking into the ambush, unprepared, possibly unarmed—at a complete disadvantage. By the time the shot is fired, the reader is in knots with anxiety. The longer you can make that foreground of anticipation, the greater the suspense. And that's what keeps the reader turning the pages—that's what puts your book on the best-seller list.

The vital thing is to approach the material and the reader with respect. I'm not slumming when I write suspense novels. I'm not a frustrated creative genius knocking off junky plots on the side while I secretly write a "real" novel. Many of our great writers have worked in this genre before me, and more will follow. It offers ample room for my creative impulses. So if I'm dissatisfied with something I've written, I don't let it pass. I throw it out and start over. It hurts like the devil, but it pays off in writing quality and self respect. If I care, I can't cheat.

To write a really successful suspense novel is more than enough challenge for me. To make a career out of writing them is more than enough reward for my having lived.

A good book means good characterization. And I never find that easy. So—I usually write biographies of my major characters. That is, I get to know so much about each one (he *tells* me, honest) that I realize I'd better write it down, so that I don't forget it. Good characters are haunted by the past just as real people are. They have flaws. They have fears. And they have personal problems unrelated to the plot, just as real people do—broken love affairs, bankruptcies, unfaithful spouses, shameful deeds they wish to forget. And their pasts, just as with real people, affect their current behavior. Character is plot—or plot is character in action. I feel that the most powerful plots are based on characters in conflict with themselves. In *Catch Me: Kill Me,* Charlie Brewer is terrified of heights. But to get what he desperately wants, he has to go down the side of a skyscraper in a bosun's chair in a fog, guided by an elderly alcoholic. In *The Trade,* Colin Thomas, suffering from claustrophobia, has to crawl through a sewer pipe underground. In both cases, the character is in conflict with himself—with his fears.

A novel is an inert lump until the character comes to life. I sit there seeing only a black silhouette, until one day he stirs and stands up, the light falls on his face, and there he is— Charlie Brewer or Colin Thomas, walking straight into a story—and I'm off on another adventure. And I'm on a new one right now. A thousand words a day: I have to get to work.

12 OF SPIES AND STORIES

by *Paul Henissart*

IT WAS Mark Twain who observed that it is not indispensable to be dead—or even an undertaker—to describe a funeral. By the same token it is not necessary to be a spy to write a spy story. Indeed, a case can be made out that it does not help much.

Some career intelligence officers aspire to be writers of spy fiction. They write urbane operational reports but often they are ill at ease with the task of crafting fiction. It is one thing to keep a Division Chief at Langley* mollified by one's prose; it's another to try to please all those potential readers out there.

In my view, the reason for this is that spies' professional activities recounted factually, without verve or relief, make for sluggish reading; some intelligence reports are more tedious than alumni bulletins. A number of years ago, I had access to some classified reports about a Polish husband-and-wife spy team who ran breathtaking risks at the outbreak of World War II and incurred atrocious punishment when they were uncovered by the Nazis. It was a grim tale, but the language in the reports was so bureaucratic, the style so leaden, the facts so unimaginatively marshaled that none of the spine-tingling tension and anguish the pair actually underwent seeped through: It all seemed unreal, and I had continuously to make

*CIA headquarters.

an effort to remind myself that the events described had, in effect, taken place.

With talent or luck, fiction sets the balance right by depicting what might have been—or better still, what almost is, in such a vivid and original way that it becomes plausible. To what degree the writer accomplishes this is a measure of his skill.

In the case of spy stories, a writer recreates a clandestine world with whose day-to-day workings most readers are unfamiliar but about which they assume a great deal. It's a world where impossible missions and dirty tricks are expected to proliferate. On this superficial level, spy fiction is escapist reading with its feet on the ground, or, if one prefers, in the mud.

But to succeed on another, more serious level—to be more than a comic strip posing as a novel—a spy story should preferably introduce us to human beings who are spies or intelligence officers but who, if things had worked out differently and destiny had operated with less or more inspiration, would be insurance salesmen or conglomerate buccaneers.

John le Carré stands head and shoulders above current writers of spy fiction on both sides of the Atlantic for two reasons. First and foremost, he draws portraits of men and women whose tastes and prejudices transcend (but often determine) the business at hand. And he draws them with a novelist's perceptive eye. In *Tinker, Tailor, Soldier, Spy,* his pastiche of the Philby case, there is a sentence which describes the upper-class hero's clothes as being "costly, ill-fitting and extremely wet." An Englishman I know, a former staffer of M1-6, was delighted by this sentence. Note that the adjectives have nothing at all to do with espionage. But my acquaintance thought (and I agreed with him) that this touch admirably contributed to the hero's credibility.

Then, le Carré is concerned with espionage as one thread

in the social fabric. No other spy writer I know of has so meticulously delineated the chummy relationship between Oxbridge dons and the British Secret Service, one talent-scouting for the other, the latter's attitudes colored by the former.

In the work of first-rate spy writers, there are recurring bonuses of this sort—familiarity with intelligence services and their foibles, the deft rendering of place, atmosphere, and language, the witty reporting of human fallibility.

Realism and research

Today's spy stories undoubtedly require a high degree of realism and precision. Readers to whom they are addressed are better informed than in the past, a fact which an author should look upon with satisfaction: it is no challenge to write for the uninformed. It follows that just as a book about painters should not confuse gouache with aquarelle technique, in a spy story terms like "contract agent," "support," and "project money" should be used knowledgeably. A case officer, if the story deals with French Intelligence, is an *officier traitant*. The British equivalent of a CIA chief of station is station commander.

One best-selling woman writer of spy fiction, continues with no discernible effect upon her popularity to refer (wrongly) to *Army* Intelligence. This outfit, according to her, invariably entangles clean-minded WASPS, who are traveling through picturesque Continental landscapes, in situations as suspenseful as a week of church socials. Her appeal is obviously to a readership that is prepared to believe anything—that the Mafia is not as bad as it is made out to be, that film producers rate art above box-office receipts, that there is a Santa Claus.

Since spy stories do tend to be set abroad (though there is no reason they couldn't occur in New Orleans or Washington, D.C.), the travel boom puts a writer on his mettle. People who have been to Vladivostok, far from being turned off by a thriller which has that city as a setting, relish reading about it. But the writer had better go there too and get his local color right. Years ago a school textbook I owned represented the French as "a light-hearted people fond of dancing in the streets." Anyone who tries to fob this off on a reader who has just jetted into present-day Paris, where dancing in rush-hour traffic might well be a death-defying act, is on the way to losing his credibility.

First-hand observation of foreign locales is a must. Budapest is not interchangeable with Bucharest. If one has never entered a Paris discotheque, how can one describe it convincingly? I set my novel, *The Winter Spy,* in Hamburg. This choice was arbitrary. It could as easily have been another West German city. However, I had stayed in Hamburg several times, was acquainted with its topography, and thought that I would relish describing it more than, say, Frankfurt. Nevertheless, a problem arose with one passage where the protagonist eludes two legmen by dashing into the Hamburg Fine Arts Museum, where I had never set foot. To write this scene, I spent a Sunday morning in that museum, looking at the pictures and puzzling out how a man on the run would get out of the building unobserved. Writing is lonely, excruciating work but field-researching a spy story is sometimes fun.

It can also provide disconcerting windfalls. While in Hamburg, I asked a German journalist to arrange a meeting for me with an inspector of the State Criminal Police. The latter, hostile on principle to writers seeking information, refused at first, then agreed with reluctance. When I entered his office and announced that I was planning to describe the murder of a high-ranking U.S. diplomat in the Municipal Park, his suspiciousness notably intensified.

"It's for a novel," I said. He glared at me in silence.

Finally, he furnished some police-procedural information that was as humorless as the man himself and later proved worthless. The meeting remained stiff throughout. I had knocked at the wrong door. But I did come away with material to set another scene in a German police inspector's office.

The real stuff of espionage is, of course, sordid. How could it be otherwise when money, blackmail and simmering resentment are so often the motivating factors? The chronic violence connected with intelligence missions is as unlovely as a war between street gangs, which they resemble. Indeed, espionage was once characterized as "a fight going on in the back alleys of the world." The Soviet's secret service operation's utter ruthlessness is notorious; The French and American services are little better. A friend of mine employed by the CIA was, upon returning to the States, threatened with painful physical retaliation if he ever opened his mouth about an operation in Italy. The *barbouzes*, the spooks recruited by de Gaulle's government during the Algerian War, who used to gather at the Don Camillo bar on Paris's Left Bank, were thugs who would pistol-whip a suspect as casually as they sipped an aperitif.

Furthermore, far from being strapping James Bonds, real-life spies and agents not only are often short of stature (to render surveillance more difficult), but they are also frequently grubby and, by accident or design, unimpressive. One fellow I knew bragged of having participated in the disposal of a Russian agent by shoving him overboard one night from the Dieppe-Newhaven car ferry. For all I know, his story had a basis in truth, but he wore elevator heels, drank milk at his company's cafeteria and cut a far more sinister figure as office politician than as hit man.

Perils, adventures—and knights-errant

Out of such material how can one create a readable, salable book? At the outset, the term "spy story" can be a pitfall. Spy fiction naturally deals with spies, but it is not really about the craft of spying at all. Successful espionage by definition is a low-profile, generally long-range business. The facts of Guillaume's career as the spy in Chancellor Willy Brandt's closet would hardly furnish the makings of a fast-paced thriller: indeed, weeks certainly went by with Guillaume communicating his reports to East Berlin as routinely as a postal clerk weighing registered mail.

It's my feeling that modern readers care very little about one basic plot assumption—an intelligence operation's purpose. Will the protagonist filch Plan X or prevent it from falling into the opposition's hands? Or will that secret shipment of enriched uranium arrive safely or not? Such conceits underlie all the heavy breathing, expensive travel, and terse dialogue, but in themselves they arouse scant excitement. In medieval ballads, the damsel sequestered in the keep and the search for the Holy Grail constituted similar devices: They were accepted for what they were, but what listeners found compelling were the perils and adventures that befell the knight-errant on his journeys. This is still largely true. In Charles McCarry's *The Miernik Dossier,* suspense springs from the intricate relationship between the members of rival intelligence services who are scrambling in Miernik the Pole's wake and the vicissitudes they face in the Sudan. Miernik's game itself is secondary, and the author shrewdly refrains from dispelling the ambiguity that envelops it.

Like all superior fiction, good spy stories have one major asset—strong characters. Whether you like or loathe them is immaterial. A reader will keep turning the pages over if he believes he is getting under the skin of a fascinating character (in real life it isn't so easy). And the more freely a writer's creative ability manifests itself with respect to his inventions, the livelier the result is likely to be.

In *The Winter Spy,* I drew on my personal experience at Radio Free Europe. McGuire the expatriate American journalist was based on a fellow worker of mine; in fact, however, he was not American, never spent a day in Budapest (in those times that entailed automatic arrest by the Hungarian authorities), did not share his apartment with an Austrian starlet, and certainly was never recruited by the CIA. But his determination to remain in Vienna after leaving Radio Free Europe was much like McGuire's in the book. I mention this simply to illustrate the extent to which fiction seizes upon a person in real life, tosses and overturns him and bears him away toward an unpredictable destination as irresistibly as does a flood.

Exploiting chance

Probably no book gets written save for a strange alliance between industry and inspiration. But inspiration is sometimes a matter of recognizing opportunity. In *Narrow Exit,* my first novel, the figure of Max Weissenberg, the commando leader, was suggested by a well-known Israeli blockade runner who had a turbulent career in the Haganah and whom I met while covering the Suez War. When I set about writing the book more than a decade later, I was unable to go to Israel. To check some details, I went to see an Israeli intelligence agent in Paris. He was a small, chunky, incredibly tough man who rented a dingy apartment, where, on overcast winter afternoons, he generously dispensed whisky and information. Several further meetings took place, and as I got to know him better, his traits and views increasingly dominated my portrait. of Max Weissenberg, superseding my earlier impressions of the blockade runner which had faded and grown unreliable with time. And one December day, it was my Paris source who helpfully proposed Max's nickname, the Hound of Lebanon. I can't help but feel that I was well advised to exploit chance at that point rather than stick obdurately to my initial idea.

Wherever possible here, I have shied away from the term "thriller," which, to my mind embraces a wider category of fiction than spy stories. Both, however, have one element in common, a sequence of swift-moving developments. This calls for careful structuring, or trouble and rewriting loom ahead. Especially in tackling double agents and double cros-ses, it is clear that without a detailed outline a writer can stray perilously far afield. Somewhere an attentive senior editor is forever ready to remark, "I find the story line gripping, but how could So-and-so have thought this *before* he knew that?"

Clichés should be avoided like poison ivy. Let's have a moratorium on renegade scientists, svelte temptresses, and would-be world conquerors. The intelligence world is baleful enough without them. Pratfalls and cosmic pronouncements are hazardous. So is facile overreliance on sex and violence—they are no guarantee to success in a market where there is a glut of both.

13 RESEARCHING AND WRITING THE CRIME BOOK— FACT OR FICTION

by *Clark Howard*

IF A WRITER is fortunate enough to get in on an actual story at its inception, he can then "live" it as he writes it—and it makes no difference whether he is writing a factual account or novelizing it. If one is not fortunate enough to be there when the event is happening, then no matter how he intends to recount the story, as fact or fiction, he must, like an historian, start digging into the past.

It was very much the latter case for me when I decided in 1976, after ten novels, to write my first true-crime book. Titled *Six Against the Rock,* it was the story of an unsuccessful prison break which took place on Alcatraz, *thirty years earlier*! It had been a spectacular affair: Six long-term convicts, after failing to get off the island, captured the main cellhouse and held it for forty-two hours against prison guards, FBI men, San Francisco police, California state troopers, the Navy *and* the Marines, while most of San Francisco watched from shore. I had no idea when I began the project of the enormous amount of research I would have to do. Had I been the least bit perceptive, I would have realized what lay ahead of me by the simple fact of what interested me in the story in the first place: No two versions of the episode were the same. The press told one story, the U. S. Bureau of Prisons another, the

National Park Service (which conducts tours of the once in-famous "Rock") another, and several chroniclers of the event who were there at the time gave their own biased versions (this latter group included former warden James "Saltwater" Johnston on one side, Robert "Birdman" Shroud on the other).

Digging for the facts

It occurred to me that, aside from Stroud, no other convict had been asked or permitted to tell what went on *inside* the cellhouse after the six convicts captured it. (In those days, the press was not allowed contact with Alcatraz prisoners, all mail was severely censored, all visits strictly monitored.) I thought if I could get in touch with some of those men, they might, after thirty years, be willing to talk to me. In taking steps to locate them, I was to learn my first hard lesson about crime research: *Forget about getting any help from the U. S. Government.* In eighteen months of trying—numerous expensive long-distance telephone calls, many letters directed to many people, hours of wasted labor—I obtained not one scrap or shred of usable information from anyone in the federal government.

Having recognized early on the federal attitude, I took another route. I composed the following classified ad, and ran it in the "Personal" column of metropolitan newspapers across the country:

ALCATRAZ. Writer wishes to contact former inmates of Alcatraz federal prison. Write Clark Howard, etc.

The response, to my delight, was considerable. Subse-quently through correspondence with those who had been on the Rock during the break, I learned, via letters, phone calls, and cassette tapes, things never before made public. I became friends with men who had known or had been America's most notorious outlaws of the twenties and thirties; men like Machine Gun Kelly and Doc Barker, who were dead; and Floyd Hamilton, Basil "The Owl" Banghart, Freddie Hunter, Volney Davis, Willie Radkay, and Dale Stamphill, who were still living. Through them, I traced others who were neutral enough to have *unbiased* (very important!) recollections of the riot: Father Joe Clark, the Rock's chaplain for seventeen years; Machine Gun Kelly's youngest son, who has become a close friend; the widow of Dr. Louis Roucek, the Alcatraz psychiatrist; and a number of others who were there at the time. With their help and generosity, I was able to tell for the first time what I believe to be the only *complete* story of the 1946 siege of Alcatraz—*Six Against the Rock*.

Fictionalizing true crime

The true story of the Alcatraz break was not my first experience in researching crime, however. Two years earlier, I had written a novel entitled *Mark the Sparrow*, which was a fictionalization of the Caryl Chessman case. There aren't many crime readers—fact *or* fiction—who are not familiar with the case of the notorious "Red Light" bandit-rapist who, after waging a twelve-year battle to avoid it, died in California's gas chamber in 1960. There was, and still is, much controversy about the Chessman case. Most of it can be included in one of two categories: (1) was Chessman, in fact, innocent of the crimes, as he maintained to the end; and (2) was the death penalty too severe in light of the fact that he had not taken a life (he was convicted under the "Little Lindbergh" law for kidnapping several female victims and forcing them to perform sex acts which resulted in bodily harm; one of the victims is still confined to a mental hospital).

There was no doubt in my mind that the Chessman story was the foundation for a good book: I had to decide whether to make it fiction or nonfiction. Several good nonfiction books had already been written on the case, leaving little if anything factually new to write about. But if I *fictionalized* it, if I put it in *novel* form, there would be plenty of *new* material to include: speculative material, could-have-happened material, and my own conclusions about much of what had been previously written.

I decided to write the book as a novel. Caryl Whittier Chessman became Weldon Carpenter Whitman, and I was off and running—or rather, off and *researching*. The fact that I was going to fictionalize the case did *not* mean that I could simply make everything up. On the contrary, it meant that I had to know just as many details as I would if I were writing a nonfiction account, because you cannot fictionalize a fact unless you are first familiar with that fact. For half a century, writers novelizing true-crime cases have found that to be true. Theodore Dreiser, researching his classic, *An American Tragedy,* learned and followed exactly the details of the 1908 Chester Gillette murder case. As did Meyer Levine in fictionalizing the 1924 Loeb-Leopold case in *Compulsion.*

So the lesson to be learned as far as research is concerned is that, whether a writer goes the fiction or nonfiction route, it is *essential* to know the facts. This rule would serve me very well writing my next book, *The Hunters,* a police procedural about a sniper killing Los Angeles policemen. Although *not* based on a true case, I learned very early in my first draft that I still had to have details if I wanted the story to ring true. Just *how* did a metropolitan police force investigate the killing of one of its own? How was a crime scene handled from start to finish when the killing was in a policeman's home and his family was involved? What part did the murdered officer's partner play in the manhunt? And a hundred other facts.

Again, the answer was *research.*

Interviewing convicts

Following the Alcatraz book, I found that I had the beginning of a "reputation" as a reliable crime writer, one who could be trusted by both sides: the violators of the law, as well as the enforcers. In spite of my many problems with the Bureau of Prisons and the FBI, I had, in *Six Against the Rock,* treated their people fairly and objectively. That did not change the attitude of those federal bureaus as far as cooperation was concerned, but it did eventually put me in the good graces of many *state* law enforcement agencies and departments of correction, which were of immense help to me in future books.

My next true-crime project came about through my meeting a forensic scientist for the San Francisco Police Department. He had worked on the physical evidence in the long search for and eventual trial of the infamous "Zebra" killers, four black muslims who for a period of 179 days attacked white people on the streets of the Bay City, killing fifteen of them. Through him I met the two homicide inspectors in charge of the case, and I was off and researching a new crime project.

The Zebra case was much more recent than the Alcatraz story—only six years old at the time that I began working on it—so I thought the research would be easier. I was wrong. Because of the sheer number of people involved—victims, survivors, killers, police officers, witnesses—I actually interviewed nearly *four* times as many persons as on the previous book, and had *six* times the notes. The sheer volume of paperwork to be read, digested, put in perspective, was awesome (the trial transcript alone ran 14,000 pages).

Again, to uncover persons who might have unbiased and/or previously undivulged information on the case, I ran a classified ad in the San Francisco papers:

> ZEBRA. Published author of 11 books wishes to contact anyone having previously unpublished information about the men convicted of the Zebra killings. Particularly interested in anyone who attended a loft meeting. Anonymity, confidentiality absolutely guaranteed. Communicate anonymously, on cassette, or any way you choose. Contact Clark Howard, etc.

Response to this ad was not as great as to the Alcatraz ad, but I nevertheless was able to reach several persons who had known the killers at various times during their lives, and one very important informant, who had been a Black Muslim in San Francisco and managed to drop out without being executed. And he *had* attended a loft meeting, the pep rallies where the street killers whipped their hatred for whites into a frenzy before taking to the streets.

Now for the first time in my research activities, I was going to attempt to interview men convicted of murder. Upon arrival at Folsom Prison, I found that my reputation had preceded me: *Six Against the Rock* was required reading for all new corrections officers there, because it pointed out so dramatically what could happen when guards became lax around maximum security convicts. The administration at Folsom cooperated fully in my numerous visits in the months to come.

Winning the confidence of black convicted killers who hated all "blue-eyed white devils" was another matter, however. That took a lot of time, patience, and perseverance. I started first with the one who considered himself the group's leader. It helped that I was able to deliver a personal message from his mother, to whom I had already talked. I emphasized that I only wanted to get to know him, that I would be scrupulously fair in presenting his side of the story, and that I would under no circumstance betray his confidence. I also promised, at a later meeting, to call off my search for his ex-wife in exchange for some candid answers about his co-defendants. It was here that I learned one very important element of interviewing criminals and convicts: When they will not talk about themselves, they frequently *will* discuss, at length, their peers.

Methods and procedures

After I had written two fictionalizations of actual crimes, one police procedural not based on an actual crime, and two lengthy true-crime books, I found that certain methods and procedures of researching crime had become part of my *modus operandi*. I had learned, for instance, not to depend on the cooperation of federal agencies; their common instinct was to avoid divulging *anything.* I had also learned that a simple, relatively inexpensive classified ad often yielded marvelous results in locating good, neutral sources of information. But the most important thing I learned was that a crime researcher has to be *trustworthy.* He has to play it as straight with one side (the criminals) as he does with the other (the authorities). Forget that rule just once, betray just *one* confidence, and everybody on *both* sides will know it the next day. And you'll never be an effective crime researcher again.

It was while interviewing the Zebra killers at Folsom that I got the idea for my third true-crime book, another prison-break story, this one being the abortive escape attempt of black radical George Jackson from San Quentin in 1971. In discussing the incident with Folsom corrections officers who had previously been assigned to San Quentin, I learned many things that had occurred *inside* the prison on the day of the break: How the gun smuggled in to Jackson actually made it inside by *accident;* how a guard who had his throat cut kept from bleeding to death by pressing his neck against the cold porcelain of a toilet base; and how a friendly exchange of working shifts had meant death for one officer, life for another. Interesting, ironic facts, the kind that make crime books, fiction or nonfiction, come to life. I also discovered something quite extraordinary: George Jackson and I had grown up just one block apart on Chicago's west side, he in his ghetto, I in my slum. I was naturally intrigued by that fact. But even had it not been so, I still would have researched and written the book that became *American Saturday,* because again I felt that here was a story which had never been *completely* told, from *all* sides.

Becoming involved in the Jackson story taught me another very valuable crime research lesson: Never take anyone at face value. *Never.* George Jackson is a classic example of why. In all, I traveled 3,000 miles and interviewed several scores of persons who had known Jackson. Gradually, as the pieces fell into place, I became faced with a sobering conclusion: George Jackson was not the great black revolutionist that his followers professed him to be; he was, in fact, a recalcitrant street thug, who had become a prison rapist, extortionist, and general trouble-maker, and who only redefined himself as a "black militant" as a way of justifying a decade of criminal irresponsibility.

To portray Jackson in this new light, I knew, would be contradictory to nearly everything previously written about him. Yet, I had to do it, *because my research dictated that I do it,* "warts and all." I did just that in *American Saturday.* One book reviewer said, "People who want to remember George Jackson as a hero won't like this book."

They didn't. But I came away with my reputation intact.

Six rules that work

In researching one of my recent crime novels, *The Wardens,* and my fact-crime book, *Brothers in Blood,* I made use of virtually everything I had learned doing the earlier books. Digging into first the history of midwestern crime, criminals, and prisons for *The Wardens,* then into the story of three brothers who had in 1973 escaped from prison in urban Maryland, fled south, and massacred a rural Georgia family (including three brothers) for *Brothers in Blood,* I automatically did the following: (1) dismissed the FBI as a source of information (though their agency was involved in both stories); (2) went directly to the state departments of correction involved (my reputation in the field of penology was again rewarded with cordial cooperation); (3) began my interviews as close to the source of pertinent information as I could (with the leader of the killer brothers, for instance), and was *absolutely honest* with everyone, every step of the way; (4) sought out as many *neutral* sources of information as I could find; (5) kept constantly alert for *unusual* facts that would give my books impact and pathos; and (6) never accepted anything at face value until the last interview was concluded, the last note taken.

Following these six rules does not, of course, have to be rigid. Some researchers, for instance, might have connections in federal agencies which will give them access to jealously guarded records; others might select stories for which it is not necessary to search for the unusual: the Charles Manson case, for example (published in the book *Helter Skelter: The True Story of the Manson Murders,* by prosecutor Vincent Bugliosi and writer Curt Gentry), about which everything is bizarre. But generally speaking, if a crime writer of fact *or* fiction is going to dig up the story himself, as opposed to "living" the story as it develops, these six guidelines will help him or her considerably.

Above all, remember the main rule: *learn the facts.*

There is no substitute for vigorous research.

14

ONE CLUE AT A TIME
by *P. D. James*

FOR ME one of the keenest pleasures of rereading my favorite mysteries is their power to transport me instantly into a familiar world of people, places and objects, a world in which I feel at once comfortably at home.

With what mixture of excitement, anticipation and reassurance we enter that old brownstone in Manhattan, that gentle spinster's cottage in St. Mary Mead (never fully described by Agatha Christie but so well imagined), that bachelor flat in London's Piccadilly where Bunter deferentially pours the vintage port [for Lord Peter Wimsey], that cozy Victorian sitting room on Baker Street.

A sense of place, creating as it does that vivid illusion of reality, is a necessary tool of any successful novelist. But it is particularly important to the fabricator of the mystery: the setting of the crime and the use of commonplace objects help to heighten by contrast the intruding horror of murder. The bizarre and the terrifying are rooted in comforting reality, making murder more believable.

There is probably no room in crime fiction that we enter with a keener sense of instant recognition than that claustrophobic upstairs sitting room at 221B Baker Street. Baker Street is now one of the dullest of London's main thoroughfares, and it is difficult, walking these wide pavements, to picture those foggy Victorian evenings with the inevitable veiled lady alighting from her hansom cab outside the door of the celebrated Sherlock Holmes.

But we can see every detail of the room into which Mrs. Hudson will usher her: the sofa on which Holmes reclines during his periods of meditation; the violin case propped against the wall; the shelves of scrapbooks; the bullet marks in the wall; the two broad windows overlooking the street; the twin armchairs on each side of the fireplace; the bottle of 7-percent-cocaine solution on the mantel shelf; the desk with the locked drawer containing Holmes's confidential records; the central table with "its white cloth and glimmer of china and metal" waiting for Mrs. Hudson to clear away.

The mental scene has, of course, been reinforced countless times in films and on television, but what is remarkable is that so vivid a picture should be produced by so few actual facts. Paradoxically, I can find no passage in the books that describes the room at length and in detail. Instead, Sir Arthur Conan Doyle builds up the scene through a series of stories object by object, and the complete picture is one that the reader himself creates and furnishes in his own imagination from this accumulation of small details.

Description, mood, and suspense

Few things reveal the essential self more surely than the rooms in which we live, the objects with which we choose to surround ourselves, the books we place on our shelves, all those small household goods that help reaffirm identity and provide comfort and a sense of security. But the description in crime fiction of domestic interiors, furnishings and possessions does more than denote character; it creates mood and atmosphere, enhances suspense and is often crucial to the plot.

In Agatha Christie, for example, we can be confident that almost any domestic article mentioned, however commonplace, will provide a clue, either true or false. A loose door number hanging on its nail; flowers that have died because no one watered them; an extra coffee spoon in a saucer; a picture postcard lying casually on a desk. In *Funerals Are Fatal,* we do well to note the bouquet of wax flowers on the malachite table. In *Murder at the Vicarage,* we can be sure that the tall stand with a plant pot standing in front of the window isn't there for nothing.

And in *The Murder of Roger Ackroyd,* we shouldn't be so intrigued by the corpse that we fail to notice how one chair has been strangely pulled out from its place by the wall.

All writers of mystery fiction use such devices, but few with such deceptive cunning. It is one of the paradoxes of the genre that it deals with that great absolute, death, yet deploys the trivia of ordinary life as the frail but powerful instruments of justice.

Because in a Christie mystery the puzzle is more important than either the characterization or the setting, she seldom describes a room in great detail. Hers is the art of the literary conjurer. How very different is the loving care and meticulous eye with which a novelist such as Margery Allingham creates for us her highly individual domestic interiors.

In *More Work for the Undertaker,* how brilliantly she describes every room of the eccentric Palinode family, so that the house itself is central to the plot, its atmosphere pervades the novel, and we feel that we know every secret and sinister corner.

But my favorite Allingham rooms are in *The Tiger in the Smoke,* with its opposing characters of the saintly Canon Avril and the psychopathic killer Jack Havoc. How simply described and how absolutely right is the Canon's sitting room. "It was the room he had brought his bride to 30 years before, and since then . . . nothing in it had ever been changed. It had become a little worn in the interim, but the good things in it, the walnut bookcase with the ivory chessmen displayed, the bureau with 13 panes in each glass door, the Queen Anne chair with the 7-foot back, the Persian rug which had been a wedding present from his younger sister, Mr. Campion's mother, had all mellowed just as he had with care and use and quiet living."

Right, too, in its very different style, is the sitting room of his dress-designer daughter, Meg, littered with its sketches of dresses and strewn with swaths of material and samples of braids and beads. "Between the damasked grey walls and the deep gold carpet there ranged every permissible tint and texture from bronze velvet to scarlet linen, pinpointed and enlivened with daring touches of Bristol blue."

This is a highly individual room in the grand manner but without pretentiousness, and I'm not in the least surprised that after a dubious sidelong glance, Chief Inspector Luke decided that he liked it very much indeed.

A room I like very much indeed is Lord Peter Wimsey's sitting room in his flat at 110A Piccadilly. We see it most clearly through the eyes of Miss Murchison in Dorothy L. Sayers's *Strong Poison*. She is shown by Bunter into a glowing, book-lined room "with fine prints on the walls, an Aubusson carpet, a grand piano, a vast chesterfield and a number of deep, cozy armchairs upholstered in brown leather.

"The curtains were drawn, a wood fire blazed on the hearth, and before it stood a table with a silver tea service whose lovely lines were a delight to the eye." No wonder Miss Murchison was impressed.

After his marriage, of course, Lord Peter honeymooned with his Harriet at Talboys, an Elizabethan farmhouse in Hertfordshire that Lord Peter bought as their country retreat, complete with inglenooked fireplace, ancient beams, tall Elizabethan chimneys, erratic plumbing and the inevitable corpse in the cellar. Meanwhile, the dowager Duchess of Denver was busying herself collecting the chandeliers and tapestries for the Wimseys' town house in Audley Square and congratulating herself that the bride "was ready to prefer 18th-century elegance to chromium tubes." I am myself partial to

18th-century elegance, but I still feel more at home in that bachelor flat at 110A Piccadilly.

Incidently, Talboys was modernized and completely refurnished, including the installation of electricity and the provision of additional bedrooms, before the murderer of its previous owner had been executed—in England a matter then of only a couple of months. That was remarkably speedy even for the 1930's. Today I am doubtful whether even the son of a Duke would be able to command such speedy service.

The ordinary made terrible

I work in the tradition of Margery Allingham and share her fascination with architecture and domestic interiors; indeed, it is often the setting rather than a particular character or a new method of murder that sparks my creative imagination and gives rise to a novel.

In my book, *The Skull Beneath the Skin,* the setting is a restored Victorian castle on a lonely, offshore island. Here the owner, obsessed with violent death, has created his own private chamber of horrors, a study decorated with old woodcuts of execution scenes, Staffordshire figures of Victorian murderers, mourning regalia and the artifacts of murder.

Here I have used the setting to fulfill all the functions of place in detective fiction: to illustrate character, create atmosphere, provide the physical clues to the crime and to enhance that sense of unease, of the familiar and ordinary made strange and terrible, which is at the heart of detective fiction.

And it is surely the power to create this sense of place and to make it as real to the reader as is his own living room—and then to people it with characters who are suffering men and women, not stereotypes to be knocked down like dummies in the final chapter—that gives any mystery writer the claim to be regarded as a serious novelist.

15 HAVE YOU TRIED MURDER?

by *Peter Lovesey*

Dear Mr. Lovesey,
I understand that you are a writer of murders. I think you will be interested to know that I have thought of a totally new and original form of murder that I am sure you could use in a book. It is simple and quite undetectable; in fact, the perfect murder. I guarantee that it will work. May I suggest that we meet for lunch in London at some mutually convenient time and place, when I am confident that we can agree on a suitable fee?

Yours in crime,
s/A.D.Z_____

When I get letters like this, I feel bound to wonder at the profession I pursue. What makes anyone into a mystery writer? An aggressive personality that needs channelling into something not too dangerous? An unhealthy interest in the macabre? Or just the hope of becoming rich and famous?

Dear Mr. Z_____,
Thank you for your offer to sell me a perfect murder. Unhappily it is of no use to me because I deal exclusively in murders that are imperfect. Otherwise the detective would never solve the crime. I am sure there must be people who would be glad to buy your idea, but if you have a conscience you will keep it to yourself.

Yours sincerely,
s/Peter Lovesey

There's a story about an old lady standing by the bookstall on a London railway station. She had been there a long time, looking more and more depressed.

A sympathetic assistant asked, "Can I help you?"

The old lady said, "I can't find anything suitable to read on the train."

"Yes," said the girl. "It's nothing but Agatha Christie—rows and rows of horrible murders."

"I know, dear," said the old lady. "I wrote them."

Dear Mr. Lovesey,

   I have just watched your television play *Waxwork*, in which the victim was poisoned with cyanide used in his photographic studio. I like nothing better than an old-fashioned murder mystery, especially a poisoning. By a strange coincidence my husband Harry's hobby is photography, but I am not sure if he uses cyanide. I had a look in the darkroom, but I couldn't see any. I wouldn't ask Harry in case he gets the wrong idea. He is an ignorant man who doesn't understand the woman's point of view, but that's another story. On another matter entirely, could you settle an argument by telling me how much cyanide is needed for a fatal dose, and if it can be detected in hot chocolate?

                          s/(Mrs.) Jane S_____

P.S. The reason is that I am writing a book.

The letters are not all so disturbing. I tell myself that the serious murderer is unlikely to betray his plans to a mystery writer. But even letters like this, which I suspect are written in fun, remind me that mine is a rather dubious area of literature. Graham Young, one of Britain's most notorious poisoners in recent years, kept a diary in which his victims' names were listed, and he claimed in his defense that they were notes for a novel he was working on.

Soon after my first mystery was published, I was invited to join a club for mystery writers. A weekend conference was announced. The agenda was formidable: a police chief on the hunt for a vicious multi-murderer; a forensic expert with a talk entitled "Every Contact Leaves its Traces"; a visit to the local police headquarters; and finally, a slide show by a Home Office pathologist. I went along out of curiosity, but in trepidation at the prospect of meeting people well-versed in ballistics, poisoning, and signs of strangulation.

I learned a lot in that weekend. The most valuable thing I

learned was not on the agenda: that mystery writers are in general inoffensive, genial, and disarming. Those I met—they included several famous and best-selling authors—admitted to some unease at being lectured on the grim realities of crime. One well-known writer of at least a dozen murder mysteries told me he would have to miss the slide show because he fainted at the sight of blood. (Several other seats were conspicuously vacant.)

When I got home, I reflected on it all. If mystery writers were reluctant to be brought face to face with death and violence, what were their books about? Was mystery fiction still as remote from harsh reality as it had been in the so-called Golden Age of Agatha Christie, Dorothy L. Sayers, and Margery Allingham?

> A drawing room, or is it a library, crowded with suspects.
> An inscrutable butler with a plateful of freshly baked scones, of the most appetizing appearance.
> "Won't you try one?" enquired Sir Jasper.
> The Inspector returned an enigmatical smile. "I have lost my appetite."
> "Oh, hell!" said Jasper forcibly. He glanced quickly to his left.
> "Watch out, Sergeant—the French windows!" snapped the Inspector.

Without detriment to the craft and ingenuity of the Golden Age writers, it is clear that the best mysteries of today are more crisply written and sharper in their observation. They are better researched, less mealy-mouthed in their accounts of violence, and more realistic in their dialogue. Yet Agatha Christie still dominates the bookstands, and Sayers, Allingham, and Ngaio Marsh still sell like the hot cakes endlessly eaten in their drawing rooms. What, I asked myself, is the secret of the enduring appeal of mysteries that established their style over half a century ago?

A game as well as a story

The first and obvious conclusion is, that like no other form of fiction, the true mystery novel presents a challenge. From the whodunits of the twenties and thirties to the whydunits and spy thrillers of more recent times, the puzzle is a principal ingredient. The best mysteries still offer readers a game as well as a story.

And what of the story? One thing can be guaranteed in mystery fiction, and is as true today as it was of the earliest Christie novels: it has the satisfying structure of a plot that is resolved. In the novel generally, there is no compunction on the writer to tell you everything that happened. How often do you hear complaints about novels that reach no conclusion whatsoever?

I think the other strong advantage of the Golden Age mysteries is that they have acquired a period charm. They are a window on a vanished age. It may be argued that they were never an accurate account of the way most people lived, but, accurate or not, those libraries and drawing rooms peopled with rich spinsters and majors and vicars and hosts of servants exist in the imagination. The values are rock solid: Right will always triumph over wrong, but what fun it will have been to have seen one of that society exposed as a blackguardly impostor!

So when I had got over my discovery that my fellow mystery writers were not ghouls, I began to understand how the best of them had adopted and adapted the real strengths of the old whodunit and created some of the most satisfying and exciting fiction being published in our time. Their concern is not with calibres of guns and temperatures of corpses; it is with the game they are playing with the reader, the need to construct a story that will work. And, most exciting, it is the opportunity the mystery gives them to describe a special world.

The possibilities are limitless. Dick Francis initiates the reader into the horse racing game; Robert van Gulik into ancient China; and Ed McBain into a tough police precinct in New York City. Within the strongly realized setting of the spy world, John le Carré explores the meaning of betrayal. James

McClure, with his Afrikaner detective and his Zulu colleague, conveys the social tensions in South African society without ever lecturing his readers. In *Stronghold,* Stanley Ellin shows a Quaker community invaded by one of its lost souls turned psychopath, and raises disturbing questions about the practicalities of faith. The mystery is not moribund; it is developing all the time. Have *you* thought of your own way of shaping its development? I hope I am persuading you to try.

My own interest is the mystery in a period setting, though I should say that I chanced on Victorian London almost accidentally. I was mainly interested in sport. It just happened that the sports event I used as background for *Wobble to Death* occurred in 1879. I am not an expert on the Victorian era, nor a history professor, just an inexhaustible collector of the trivia of times past. But, with *The False Inspector Dew,* I moved on to the nineteen-twenties, but I suppose I am still rooted in the past. Not so deeply, I hope, as this reader thought:

Dear Mr. Lovesey,
I have read all of the Sergeant Cribb books with great enjoyment, but I did not write to tell you because I thought you were dead. My husband says he thinks you may still be alive. I suppose it does not really matter, but we would be most grateful to have this matter cleared up.

Yours sincerely,
s/Jennifer Y———

Dear Mrs. Y———,
Thank you for your query as to whether I am a dead writer. I have sometimes wondered about this myself. But I cannot agree that it does not really matter. It matters to me and my wife, and my wife says she is sure I am still breathing. I hope this has cleared up the question.

Yours sincerely,
s/Peter Lovesey

16
PLOTTING SHORT MYSTERY STORIES
by *Dan J. Marlowe*

AFTER THIRTY years of plotting mystery/suspense short stories, a writer knows what has worked; more important, he knows what hasn't. The fact remains, however, that current trends in magazine fiction should induce the writer to re-examine the building blocks of his plotting structure.

With markets contracting and writers increasing, it's difficult to send an editor a short story sufficiently unique or unusual to encourage him to consider publishing it. The first idea that comes to mind may not be good enough. The second, third, or fourth may not be, either.

Some editors send guidelines that state what they are looking for. Unfortunately, guidelines are generalizations that can confuse as much as they can help. Also, despite such guidelines, an editor doesn't really know what he or she wants to buy or will buy until he has it in hand.

Headlines and plot lines

Plot lines can come from a number of places. Reading, of course. How many times have we finished reading a story and said to ourselves, "Now, if that ending were changed and that character eliminated, and that background changed . . . why, it would be a different story. A better story." And we rush to the typewriter.

Conversations, either direct or overheard from two tables away, can be helpful. Conversations are tricky, though. Unlike reading it in a story, how much of a plot twist heard in conversations can be retained? If you don't have a notebook and pencil with you, trying to recall conversations later can be frustrating, since they fade away quickly, no matter how good a writer's memory.

Television shows can provide a plot line; radio can, too, although that's less likely nowadays. But probably the most helpful aid of all in putting backspin on a story idea is the most available medium of all, the daily newspaper.

Hardly a day goes by without having something appear in the paper that will lend itself to fictional conversation. A file of newspaper clippings can go a long way to jog laggard inspiration when the plotting well runs dry, as it occasionally does for all of us.

What type of newspaper item produces story ideas?

Almost anything.

It can be a headline.

It can be the lead story of the day, a sidebar item, or a blind classified ad.

The following ad appeared recently: "A highly qualified chauffeur is needed to drive for a leading company. The right candidate will have a background in law enforcement, business driving experience, and will be articulate and well-groomed. Excellent references and the ability to work flexible hours are also required. Duties other than driving may be assigned in the corporate offices, depending upon experience and background."

The plotting mind leaps immediately into action. The company is looking for an ex-cop or ex-private eye (perhaps both in the same package). A bodyguard? The wording suggests more than that. There's a taste of something not quite aboveboard. Something a bit shady.

So the writer can take an ex-cop, ex-private eye character and send him to apply for the job to the company of the writer's choice. The character can be a burnt-out case on his current job and be looking for a change. He applies, is accepted, and at once finds himself deeper in the manure pile than he had been formerly.

It doesn't matter what the writer gives the character to do. It's sufficient that the writer has found an off-beat situation into which to insert his character. "The right candidate will be articulate and well-groomed." Hm-m-m . . . could the corporate employer be a woman? The writer's imagination has no restrictions upon it.

Sometimes a newspaper item will develop over a period of time into one or more plot twists, not immediately apparent to the writer. The story may take a direction impossible to discern at the beginning.

Recently, a salesman 75 miles from home came out of his motel room one morning, and when he got into his car, it exploded. The roof and both doors were blown away. Amazingly, the salesman walked away from the blast, his major injury a seriously scorched rear end.

The police at first concluded the car bombing was gangland connected. Extensive checking proved this to be incorrect. A parallel thought was that the salesman might have staged the bombing for his own purposes. The discovery of an unexploded pipe bomb under the car's front seat ruined that theory. One pipe bomb had gone off, one hadn't. No one could depend upon that kind of freakish incident to further a plot of one's own devising.

Time passed. Three months later the police arrested two men for the bombing, one of them a good friend of the salesman's wife. The friend insisted the wife had encouraged his activity in connection with her husband. The wife denied it. The salesman loyally supported his wife's statements.

More time passed while the police dug more deeply. The next public announcement was to the effect that the police were theorizing that the wife's friend might have done the dirty deed without the wife's knowledge to further his own relationship with her.

This was followed a week later by the police charging the wife with instigating the entire affair. She was indicted, and her boy friend and his companion agreed to testify against her. The wife protested her innocence and said that whatever her boy friend had done, he had done without her knowledge. The salesman still supported his wife.

The next time the veil was lifted, the wife was in court pleading no contest to a charge of attempted murder. In the eyes of the law, a no contest plea is the same as a guilty plea except it allows the judge more leniency in sentencing. During the wife's plea, the salesman was in court; unbelievably, he was still supporting her. The wife comes up for sentencing in three months.

Options and spin-offs

That's the end of the newspaper story, but examine the possibilities it opens up for the fiction writer. It can be written fictionally as it happened, of course, but that's only one of the options. It's true that as it happened it's bizarre enough to attract an editor's attention, but some of the possible spin-offs would be almost as attractive:

1) Instead of appearing as an innocent fool, the salesman could take the bit in his teeth and do some digging himself, which places the key information in the hands of the police. The tale can be a story of revenge.

2) Instead of the bloody and would-be bloodier circumstances of the situation, the story line could be lightened up all

along the way without the factual grimness. The story can be treated as a farce which—except for the participants—it was.

With an example like the foregoing, writers can't complain that newspapers aren't writing their stories for them. Day after day some odd item in the newspaper can be clipped and added to a writer's file. Sometimes two items can be combined to make a better fictional whole.

Sometimes the truth itself is better than fiction. An almost illiterate man served three years in jail for a warehouse robbery he insisted he didn't commit. His defense was that he was a mile away in a shopping plaza, but he had no witnesses.

Eventually, he interested a lawyer in his case, and the lawyer did some checking of his own. The man serving time had furnished a passionately detailed description of the shopping plaza where he claimed he had been, right down to a description of a pie truck, which had blocked his exit when he wanted to leave. The lawyer determined that no store in the plaza handled pies and lost his interest in the matter.

Some time later while the prisoner was watching television in the prison rec room, a commercial came on. "There!" the prisoner screamed to his befuddled fellow prisoners. He was pointing at the television screen. "There's the truck!" On the screen, an 18-wheeled behemoth was disappearing into the distance. Its rear doors were labeled "P.I.E." In smaller letters underneath, additional lettering said "Pacific Intermountain Express," a well-known trucking company.

The prisoner got in touch with the lawyer, who re-opened his inquiry. Pacific Intermountain Express log books confirmed that one of their company trucks had indeed made a call at that particular plaza at the time claimed by the prisoner. With that hinge to hang further questions on, the lawyer developed additional facts that enabled him to go back to court and ask for his client's freedom, which was granted. The "pie truck" story became a staple of prison lore and can still be heard from time to time today.

But can you imagine an editor accepting it as fiction? The editor would think it too strange, too incredible. And the offer of proof would not be likely to satisfy him. After all, having lived as long as he has, he knows the difference between truth and fiction, doesn't he?

Occasionally fact and fiction can be worst enemies.

One final note about the plotting of mystery/suspense short stories. Editorial attitudes change and must be taken into consideration. Have you as a writer ever given thought to the steadily increasing number of women editors in the magazine world? And that at least some of these women editors look with disfavor upon stories told from a male chauvinist viewpoint? It's a factor that should be seriously considered today in your plotting to increase your chances of getting your story published.

But for a beginning, start a file of newspaper clippings of the odd and bizarre of life's happenings, which, allowed to marinate, may well produce a salable story.

17

MYSTERIES WITHIN MYSTERIES

by *Patricia Moyes*

AS A WRITER of mystery stories, the compliment I treasure most is when somebody says to me, "The characters in your books are so alive. They are just like real people." I find that this is often said on a note of faint surprise, as if the personages in a detective novel had no right to be anything more than cardboard puppets, dancing through the intricacies of the plot.

I have to admit that this surprise is sometimes justified. Some mystery authors seem content to sacrifice credibility of character to the speed and thrill of the action. Others—a more distinguished group—tend to create one splendidly rounded character in the person of their detective, who recurs in book after book, but they bother very little with the personalities of the supporting cast. For me, the reality of my people is tremendously important, and I like to think that my concern for them enhances the enjoyment of my readers.

"But," you may say, "a mystery novel should be fast-moving, baffling and exciting. Who wants to take time out for in-depth character studies and long descriptions of individual characters?"

Bringing characters to life

You are quite right. A long description will never bring a character to life in the mind of the reader. So, how is it to be done?

First, by what I can only call love and concern on the author's part. You have to take the time to think about your characters, until you know them like old friends. You should explore and discover far more about them than you will ever need to use in the book. Decide not only how they look, but how they dress, what they like to eat, what books they read, what their hobbies are. Above all, listen to them until you hear their voices in your mind.

This brings me to my second point. However well you may come to know your characters, it will do no good unless you have developed a technique for communicating your knowledge to your reader through the medium of the printed page. In my view, this is best achieved by dialogue.

Many excellent prose writers go all to pieces when they try their hands at dialogue. I think this comes about because writing dialogue takes a special discipline which they have never taken the time to study. There is a world of difference between words intended to be read, and words intended to be spoken, and, whether in a play or a book, all dialogue falls into the latter class. The writing of it is a technique, and it must be learned.

I wish I could simply recommend that every writer have the good luck I had—the chance to spend years working in the theater before I ever came to novel writing. Of course, that's not possible, but there is a lot you can do.

See as much professional theater as you possibly can. Don't just sit there and enjoy yourself; bring out your analytical faculties. Read the play both before and after you see it. Learn to distinguish among the various contributions which go to make up the production—those of the writer, the actor and the director. Remember that as a novelist your job will be even tougher than the dramatist's, for you will not have the benefit of a talented interpreter—a really good actor can make magic and touch his audience with the most banal of lines. Your dialogue will have to be good enough and punchy enough to make direct contact with your readers. If possible, join an amateur dramatic group and start looking at lines from the actor's viewpoint. You will very soon discover that there is a world of difference between dialogue that reads impressively, and dialogue that plays well. A critic once said about *The Taming of the Shrew,* "It's really a terrible play. The trouble is that it plays so superbly." Read your Shakespeare again, not as great literature, but as an actor's script. *He* knew all about dialogue.

Listen to people. Listen to everyone you meet, and take time to analyze your reactions. You will find that a great many of the opinions you form of people speaking are based not on what they say, but on how they say it.

For instance, that man in the railway train the other day. You classified him at once as fussy, self-centered, and a bit of an old woman. Why? He wanted the window closed. Well, there was nothing so strange about that; you were thinking of closing it yourself. All right, think back. He was reading a newspaper, and you noticed that instead of flapping the pages around like most people, he had folded it neatly into quarters in order to read his chosen piece. Then, he was already on his feet and closing the window before he spoke, and he certainly did not request your opinion. He said, "You don't mind if we have the window closed? I'm extremely prone to chills at this time of year."

One mannerism, one short sentence—and you had made up your mind as to the sort of man he was. You'll notice that it is not necessary to describe his appearance at all. Your readers will fill in the blanks for themselves.

How very different was that woman at the cocktail party.

"I'm Amanda Bickersteth. I've been *dying* to meet you. I've read *all* your books."

"I'm so—"

"Now, you must tell me exactly how you think up all those *marvelous* plots."

"Well, as a matter of—"

"That one set on the tropical island . . . you must know the Caribbean *inside out*. Come on now, do tell—which island was it really?"

"I don't—"

"Dwight and I go to St. Thomas every winter. Oh, I know *just* what you're going to say—it *is* crowded, but we just love it. Oh, dear, there's Dwight now. I'm afraid I must rush. It's been *so* interesting talking to you, I really feel I've learned *a lot* about writing . . . ."

You get the idea? One day, both those people will find a niche in one of your books.

"Creating" a work of fiction

This is not to say that you ever can or should take a real person and "put him into a book." Unless you are writing the story of his life, he will not fit conveniently into the mold of your plot. What's more, if you have a real-life model to draw from, you will always be asking yourself, "What would my friend do in these circumstances?" rather than, "What will my imaginary character do next?"

A work of fiction is a creation, and the people in it are, literally, your creatures. The man in the train and the woman at the party are no more than raw material, jottings in a notebook. (I don't keep one myself, except mentally, but many writers do and find it very useful.) One day, when you need a social chatterbox or an egocentric hypochondriac for your story or novel, a gesture or a phrase will emerge from your memory, digested and ready for use.

To return to the subject of dialogue. I advised you to listen until in your mind you could "hear" your people talking, and this is vitally important. Speak the lines of dialogue aloud— or else imagine them spoken by your character, in his or her voice and intonation. You will very soon find yourself thinking, "No, she wouldn't put it like that. She'd come straight to the point," or, "He wouldn't be able to resist being a bit long-winded over a thing like that." This may sound too easy, but I firmly believe that if every author followed those simple rules, a lot of books would be a great deal easier to read—and a lot of good novels could be transferred to the stage or the screen without the necessity for rewriting a lot of literally unspeakable dialogue.

"Defending" your plots

When I talk about getting to know your characters, I don't mean that you should hesitate to put pen to paper until you have mentally created at least half a dozen living, credible human beings. If you tried to do that, you would probably never start to write the book at all. It is here that we come close to the heart of what will always remain a mystery to me, and, I suspect, to many other writers. Does the writing create the character, or the character the writing? At what point is a fictional personality born? When does he or she become truly alive? All I can tell you is my own experience. My books start with a background—the place, the activity, the social ambience that forms the backdrop of the story. Secondly, I have to work out the plot like a problem in logic or mathematics.

At this stage, I freely admit, the characters are very shadowy indeed—a bloodless collection labeled "rich businessman," "social climber hostess," "ambitious young journalist," and so on. A stereotyped lot, to be sure, but most of us are stereotypes to strangers, who see us only from a distance. The closer we get to other people, the more their personalities begin to emerge from behind the convenient labels.

It is the same with fictional characters. As you write, listening all the time for those voices, remembering quirks of speech or behavior from real life, you will find your people stepping out of the shadows, revealing themselves in their own true personalities. If this sounds like a sort of miracle, I can only agree that it is just that. What is more, some of the stronger-minded characters are quite capable of taking your plot and twisting it to suit their own ideas. So far, I have managed to defend my basic plot structure—the murderer, the victim, the method, the motive, and the means of discovery—against all comers, but it has not always been easy. Designated murderers have developed such charm that they have nearly succeeded in talking themselves out of just retribution; victims can turn out to be so entertaining that I can hardly bear to part with their company early in the book.

With key characters like those, the author must either harden his heart or scrap the book and start again. Once you depart from your plot structure, you are lost, and your characters will fall with you. When it comes to the minor people in the story, however, it is a different matter. They grow from chapter to chapter like ivy up a wall. They become headstrong, stubborn, talkative, and possessive. They often behave in quite unexpected ways.

In my own novel writing I have had a young woman who simply refused to marry the eminently suitable young man I'd selected for her; a harsh, unsympathetic, middle-aged husband who turned out to be deeply and movingly in love with his young wife, although he could not find the way to tell her so; a serious-minded young bureaucrat who turned out to have a wickedly mischievous sense of humor that almost wrecked my plot (I should have been warned about him, because I had met his brother in an earlier book; frivolity obviously ran in the family).

As the author, of course, I could have simply forced all these characters to behave as I had originally intended them to do. This might have made my job somewhat easier—but it would have destroyed all my satisfaction in the work, because it would have withdrawn from my creatures the fragile breath of life which I had offered them, and which they had accepted. And, for sure, nobody would ever have paid me that nice compliment, "They are just like real people."

18

THE INNER
SUSPENSE STORY

by *Marcia Muller*

BECAUSE OF its need for a strong and logical structure, the suspense novel is one of the most challenging forms of fiction. The writer must construct not one, but two series of actions: the inner and the outer story.

The outer story is the series of surface events you present to your readers. In a murder mystery, these are the apparent circumstances of the crime and the steps the detective takes to solve it. At the conclusion, the outer story joins with the inner story to form a solution.

Much like the steel girders of a building, the inner suspense story is what the outer rests upon. It is the action that occurs behind the scenes and, in many cases, years before the novel opens. Without these events, your crime has no motivation and your characters are mere cardboard figures, isolated in an improbable present without a past to lend them reality.

Every suspense novel begins with a planning phase, which is as important as the actual writing. When I began my detective novel, *Ask the Cards a Question,* I already had an investigator, Sharon McCone, whom I had created for an earlier novel. Having worked with Sharon before, I knew her and had written a five-or-six-page detailed biography prior to my first novel. But now I wanted to do more with her.

I planned to set the story in Sharon's colorful San Francisco neighborhood and use some of the unusual types who live there. In addition, I wished to bring in an old friend, Linnea

Carraway, from Sharon's high school days in San Diego. Using people and a setting that the protagonist already knows is a good choice for a beginning novelist. Most of the details of the past, which form the inner story, are already in the mind of the main character; so introducing them is simpler than if they were previously unknown.

Thus far, I had a setting: a several-block area in San Francisco's Mission district, the location of Sharon's apartment building, a corner grocery, a neighborhood tavern, and a rehabilitation center for blind people. I had two characters—Sharon and her friend Linnea.

Both the inner and the outer story stem from the characters. I had to add other characters and define who they were. What were the relationships among them? Since I was writing a mystery, a few characters had to have illicit secrets and an urgent need to hide them.

Since there was a grocery store in the neighborhood, why not a grocer? Mr. Moe, an Arab with a past. The rehabilitation center would have a director—Herb Clemente, also a man with secrets. And there was Sebastian, the blind man who delivered brushes made at the center. Other tenants in Sharon's building—Madame Anya, the fortune–teller; Molly, the proverbial good neighbor; Molly's estranged husband, Gus—rounded out my cast of characters.

For each character I wrote a brief biography. These did not need to be as detailed as Sharon's; a few paragraphs would do. In each, I outlined basic background, principal physical and behavioral traits, and a dark secret, if any. From the physical and behavioral traits, I selected one or two to emphasize in describing the person.

The catalytic event—story trigger

Now I was ready to begin mapping out the inner story. The plot, of course, begins with a catalytic event that triggers the action: in this case, a murder. Whose?

Again I chose a character who could easily be described because she was someone Sharon knew: Molly, the woman who took in packages from the mailman for the other tenants and baked cookies at Christmas. This choice had as an added advantage the fact that Molly was a likable person whose murder the reader would want to see solved.

At this point, it is a good idea to pose your central question, and to do so as clearly as possible. Mine was: "Someone has strangled Molly Antonio in her apartment. Who did it, and why?"

To answer, I visualized the murder scene. Molly is lying on a blue rug in the living room; the police officers have put a sheet over her. What else? A bag of groceries has been overturned. The phone has been knocked off the hook. Drawers have been ransacked. The murder weapon is a piece of cord, very much like the cord Sharon cut off when she threaded the rod for her new curtains the other day. When last seen that cord was in her apartment.

Groceries, I thought. What if Molly did all her shopping at Mr. Moe's grocery store? What if she had been there that evening? What if she had gone there for more than groceries? The drapery cord. What if the segment that Sharon cut off really was missing from her apartment? What if she questioned her houseguest, Linnea, about it, and Linnea seemed evasive? What if . . . ?

After keeping some possibilities and discarding others, I was able to decide on a killer and construct the inner story. I found it useful to summarize this story in two or three pages, which I used for reference later when I couldn't remember the exact date such-and-such took place.

As you construct the inner story, your secondary characters will develop more fully—often surprisingly. I found that Madame Anya, the fortune-teller on the third floor, had an estranged husband whom Sharon didn't know. And, in turn, the husband had a police record. Mr. Moe, the grocer, had a tragic past. Sebastian, the brush salesman, had a penchant for playing the ponies. My characters had become as shady a lot of folks as you could hope to meet, and I had to revise my biographies accordingly. After that I was ready to proceed with my plot chart.

The plot chart is a useful tool for a beginning writer. In time—as I have—you'll find your plotting is better if you exercise more spontaneity than the chart allows, and then it will become unnecessary. But it was invaluable to me for working out my first three novels.

The chart takes the form of a grid. Down the left-hand side I leave space for the day and time. Across the top I list the characters: detective first, killer next, so their movements are easy to compare. In the columns under each character, I note where they are and what they are doing at every moment of the action. The plot chart begins where the inner story begins, and I list all relevant events up to the start of the novel. Once the story is underway, I break the entries down into chapters, specifying the span of time covered in each. Again, this provides a good reference for the point at which you want your sleuth to say, "I found the body last . . ." You can quickly check the chart and finish with "Thursday."

Flashbacks

Introducing the inner story in a manner that seems natural and nonintrusive is often difficult for the beginning novelist. Fortunately, there are many technical devices that can facilitate this.

The most common of these is the flashback. The flashback actually takes your reader into a scene from the past. The scene in itself is not particularly difficult to write, but getting in and out of a flashback scene without confusing the reader can be tricky. In *Ask the Cards a Question,* I wanted to show Mr. Moe, the grocer, as he was when Sharon first saw him. To set this up, I showed Sharon in the store, watching the grocer and thinking back to this occasion. She says:

> *The first time I'd ever* come into the store, *I'd* gotten a loaf of bread and approached the counter in time to observe the grocer close in on a neophyte delinquent bent on stealing candy from a glass jar by the cash register.

The words I have italicized in this example tip off the reader (as does the past perfect tense in "I'd") that we have gone into the past. To return to the present Sharon says, "*Now* Mr. Moe handed me coffee and leaned against the counter, cup between his slender hands." "Now" or similar words easily tell the reader that we have come back to the main action.

Another way to introduce the past is to set up a situation that makes your narrator think about prior events. In the beginning of *Ask the Cards a Question,* I needed to characterize Linnea Carraway, a woman with a drinking problem brought on by a divorce. I also needed to point up Sharon's long friendship with her, which would explain why Sharon put up with Linnea's destructive behavior.

I decided to have Sharon return home after a long day. She is tired and looking forward to a cool glass of wine. In her apartment, she finds wet towels strewn on the floor, an unmade bed, dirty dishes piled in the sink, and no wine—Linnea has drunk it all. She leaves in disgust, but soon realizes she doesn't know where she is going, and sits down on the front steps, saying to herself, "I should think . . ." She goes on:

> But what was there to think about? Linnea Carraway, my oldest friend, had turned into an obnoxious self-centered bitch . . . Not even my fondest memories of the days when we were growing up together in San Diego could change the facts of Linnea's drastic deterioration.

Then, making the memory more vivid:

> Even now, my mind traveled to San Diego, to my bedroom in my parents' old, rambling house, to a younger Linnea, sitting crosslegged on the floor as she dealt out a single game of solitaire.

Again, as with the flashback, I brought Sharon out of her reflective mood with the use of the word "now."

In the suspense novel, it is important to introduce information from the inner story that provides clues or is crucial to the solution of the crime without making the clues obvious. One method of doing this is to have a character express what seems to be idle curiosity about something that is apparently irrelevant. To bring out a crucial fact about Molly, the murder victim, I had Sharon casually ask Molly's husband a question, following it up with the thought, "I knew very little of my dead neighbor's past."

Offhand comments also serve the same purpose. At one point, Linnea reports to Sharon that Molly had told her:

> . . . she wished she'd never seen the cards. Christ, Sharon, it was just some stupid, superstitious thing. Why am I supposed to remember?

Because of Linnea's attitude, Sharon discounts what may be a valuable clue.

Finally, the past may be introduced in a purely factual way. Obviously a direct question always works. For example, Sharon asked her apartment manager something that she had been wondering about, and he answered her. I also made use of her boss, Hank Zahn, who was an information freak and saved old newspapers and magazines. When Sharon mentioned a certain subject to him, because of his enthusiasm for his periodical collection, he dug out an article and read it to her. The information later linked up with a clue she discovered elsewhere.

The key to bringing in the past without overwhelming your reader is to sprinkle it throughout your entire novel, a bit at a time, using a mixture and variety of the devices described above.

Obviously, not all the steps I went through in writing *Ask the Cards a Question* are necessary for every writer or for every novel. Some writers keep the inner story in their heads, while others may require far more than two or three pages to summarize it. Many will need only the sketchiest of plot outlines, while others will want to use a chart plotted down to the hour. Whatever approach you take, however, if you know your inner story backward and forward, you will be well on your way to constructing an edge-of-the-chair suspense novel.

19 VERISIMILITUDE IN THE CRIME STORY

by *Al Nussbaum*

I WAS SITTING at one of the four-place tables in the mess hall of the U.S. Penitentiary, Leavenworth, Kansas. My two companions were serving sentences for violations of narcotics control laws. Throughout the meal, they talked about places they had been, drugs they had used, and times they had been arrested or had somehow avoided it. Then, as we were getting up to leave, one casually asked the other: "By the way, who was your connection in St. Louis?"

The second man set his tray back on the table and glared angrily. It looked as though there might be a taboo against asking the name of a drug supplier. "Who was my connection in St. Louis?" he asked, as though trying to make sense of an idiot's babbling. *"Who* was my connection? In St. Louis—" he pounded his chest once "—*I* was the connection!"

Besides illustrating the fact that no one, regardless of his situation, wants to be put on the bottom, this incident has another point to make: prisons *are not* full of men claiming to be innocent. Though movies, TV, books and magazines are always depicting convicts as men who fervently deny any wrongdoing, just the opposite is true. Prison, like every society, has a social structure, a pecking order, but its values are reversed. At the top of the prison social ladder are the big-time swindlers and bank robbers; at the bottom are the petty thieves and sexual deviates. A man who claimed to be innocent would find he had no standing at all.

I'm sure most convicts play down their offenses when talking to officials and outsiders, but they seldom do so among themselves. I've heard hundreds of prisoners brag about what they got away with, but I've never heard one claim that the police had arrested the wrong man. In fact, it's not uncommon for a car thief or check passer to pretend he's a bank robber in an effort to gain more acceptance.

Realistic details and facts

This is just one example of how the verisimilitude, the illusion of reality a writer creates by carefully weaving realistic details and interesting facts into his work, is often flawed in crime stories. Almost every writer tries his hand at a crime story sooner or later, but few seem to give much thought to the special hazards they face. As a result, many writers have unknowingly included inaccurate details or completely false "facts."

Since few writers have firsthand knowledge of police procedures and criminal operations, they must depend upon research for details. One writer's error can find its way into print so many times that it becomes generally accepted as true. That's how the prison-is-full-of-innocent-men cliché came into being, and that's how many others are being perpetuated. Unfortunately, it takes only one small error, if detected by the reader, to destroy an otherwise perfect illusion of reality.

Once this danger is recognized, the solution becomes obvious: a crime story should be researched in exactly the same way as any other piece of fiction. A writer should not use fiction as a source of "facts" for a crime story any more than *Lost Horizon* would be used as a source of facts about the Himalayas, or the Doctor Kildare books as a source of medical data. The best place to go for information is always to an expert who has the answers you want or to a non-fiction book on the subject. And, if a writer is ever tempted to use something he has read about in a fictional piece, or seen on TV or in the movies, he should check it carefully first. Anything that can't be confirmed shouldn't be used.

Striking a balance

The goal of the crime story is the same as for all other commercial fiction—to entertain. It accomplishes this goal, or fails to, in the same way all commercial fiction does—by the various balances it maintains, or fails to maintain. The writer uses bits of reality to build an illusion of reality. He must balance his cold facts with skillful plotting and believable characters. Just as it is important to attain a balance between too much dialogue and not enough, and too much exposition and not enough, it is important, in crime fiction especially, to find a balance between too much detail and not enough.

The crime writer *is not* trying to teach anyone anything, least of all how to commit a crime. In fact, since the theme of crime fiction is most often *Crime Does Not Pay,* any effort of the writer toward Fagin-like teaching would be self-defeating. Instead, just as he must find and hold the balance between too much detail as a whole and not enough, he should give only that amount of criminous detail necessary to establish verisimilitude, without seeming to be instructive.

This last is easier to accomplish than it sounds; for once every effort has been made to include only factual detail, no reader, no matter how knowledgeable, can find blunders that will shatter the illusion and his faith in the writer's expertise. After that, a minimum of criminous detail is all that is needed.

The greatest threat to a crime writer's verisimilitude is his own memory. Crime fiction is written by people who like to read it. Consequently, many writers have a storehouse of "facts" that simply aren't so. And, just as we will continually misspell some words until the error is pointed out, the writer will repeat these facts until he has some reason to doubt their accuracy.

Repeating errors

I've seen some errors many times. For instance, we have all read or heard about wax impressions. I can't count all the times I have read about someone jamming soft wax into a lock and removing a perfect likeness of the lock's key. Sometimes, through the miracle of movies and TV, I've even seen it done. Unfortunately, it's impossible. If it weren't, all locks would have been replaced by armed guards long ago. This story probably got its start around the turn of the century. At that time, one of the most common locks had a huge weakness. It was discovered that if a blank key were dipped in hot wax to give it a thin coating, and then inserted into the lock, the wax would pick up impressions of the lock's wards, showing where to file to make a key. Because of this lack of security, these warded locks have long since been replaced by Yale-type pin-tumbler locks in most cases, but crime fiction inherited the wax impression.

Speaking of locks and keys, writers often make a couple of other errors. It takes two hands to pick a lock. If a character does it while holding a flashlight, he'll have to hold the light with his teeth. Also, "skeleton" keys are not used in pin-tumbler locks. "Master" keys, "pass" keys, "try" keys, yes, but not "skeleton." Like the man who says "hep" instead of "hip," the author who writes about "skeleton" keys dates himself.

Another thing we've all read about or seen in movies is safe manipulation. The burglar or detective, hero or villain, presses his ear to the door of a safe, gives the combination dial a few turns, and *presto!* the door swings silently open. Although it is possible to manipulate some combination locks quite easily, none of the descriptions of it that I've seen come close to the reality. For one thing, the tumblers of a safe are flat, disc-shaped pieces, each with a notch along its outer edge. As the dial is turned, these tumblers are rotated. When they are lined up properly, the safe can be opened. The tumblers of a safe do not drop or fall anywhere; therefore, hearing plays no part in manipulation. Keen eyesight and a sensitive touch are necessary, however, so it's unlikely anyone would attempt manipulation with a flashlight as the only source of illumination, or while wearing gloves. And, contrary to every description I've seen, it's the *last* number of the combination that is discovered first, followed by the next-to-last number, and so on.

I suppose someone might say the details of safe manipulation were probably distorted on purpose some time in the past to keep knowledge out of the wrong hands, but I doubt that is the reason. Everything I've just written is as accurate as I can make it, but no one could hope to open a safe with only the information I've given. Most writers pride themselves on their realism. I believe that false facts and inaccurate details are usually the result of misinformation and faulty research, not an intentional act of the writer.

Of course, the examples I have given aren't likely to be noticed by the average reader—both prison life and locksmithing are fairly esoteric subjects. That probably explains why these errors have gone unchallenged as long as they have.

The facts of firearms

On the other hand, the United States is one of the more gun-conscious countries, and even those who don't own firearms and haven't handled them, know how they operate—everyone, it seems, except crime writers. As in the case of locks and safes, crime writers' knowledge of handguns is often tied to a fifty-year-old technology, or else a nonexistent one.

Automatic pistols and revolvers are both handguns, but that is about the only similarity between them. A revolver has a cylinder that swings out for loading and unloading. As the trigger is pulled or the hammer cocked, the cylinder rotates, lining up a new firing chamber with the barrel. An automatic on the other hand is much flatter than a revolver and is usually made ready for firing by inserting a loaded magazine (*not* a clip!) into the hollow handgrip. Although most automatic pistols have one or more safety catches, revolvers do not. There is no well-known revolver equipped with a manual safety. What appears in photographs to be a safety catch on the left side of many revolvers is actually the cylinder release. Also, the practice of leaving an empty chamber under the hammer of a revolver went out with Jesse James, or very nearly so. Modern revolvers have safety features incorporated into their designs that make this precaution unnecessary.

There is one other difference between automatics and revolvers that crime writers seem unaware of—despite the special effects produced by TV and movies, revolvers cannot be silenced effectively. Hiram Maxim patented the first firearm silencer back about the time he perfected smokeless powder, and there have been many new and improved designs since then, but none of them will work on a revolver. All firearm silencers operate by reducing the sound of the weapon's report which is caused by the rapid release of powder gases. Revolvers have a slight space between the cartridge cylinder and the barrel. Noise-producing gas is able to escape at this point, and so, revolvers cannot be silenced effectively. Here again, accuracy does not require that a writer give the construction details of a silencer, any more than it was necessary to give a graphic description of manipulation. If anything, the use of only accurate details should allow the writer to produce the desired effect with a minimum number of them.

Stories for entertainment

Other than through carelessness, there is one other way that crime writers sometimes flaw their stories—they sometimes forget their goal is entertainment and try to hit their readers over the head with a club-like message. In one of his last books, Raymond Chandler introduced a character whose sole purpose seemed to be to voice the author's personal opinions, and the story came to an abrupt halt while he did it. I've always seen this as an example of one time a master of the crime genre made a mistake; but in recent years I've read short stories that by comparison make Chandler's puppet character seem a very subtle device.

After the Supreme Court handed down its *Miranda* v. *Arizona, Escobedo* v. *Illinois,* and other decisions in the areas of representation and procedure, newspapers and magazines carried numerous articles both pro and con. Soon after that, there were many stories published that were complete distortions of the legal process. The actual effect of these decisions was far less than either supporters or detractors had expected. Most recent decisions in these areas have not been ruled retroactive; a man in prison cannot use them to effect his release. And in only two cases was the Court's decision instrumental in the release of the man who had brought the original action. The Court reaffirmed existing law that had been ignored; but, except for setting guidelines for the future, a favorable decision resulted only in a new trial for a man, not freedom.

In the case of the stories that showed blood-stained murderers being released on technicalities, I think the authors' propagandizing hurt the stories more than any simple inaccuracy might have done. If a writer has a gripe, if something is bothering him, if he feels the urge to climb upon a soapbox, he should write an article.

20 PLOT VERSUS CHARACTER IN THE MYSTERY

by *Lillian O'Donnell*

As SOON AS someone finds out I'm a writer the first question he invariably asks is: "What do you write?"

"Mysteries," I tell him.

His eyes dull; his lip curls. "I never read mysteries." He barely conceals his disdain.

"Try them; you'll like them," is my standard reply. The other day, however, having said it and started to move on, I was stopped by his next remark.

"All mysteries are the same. Well, they are. A crime is committed, then it's solved. Right? Simple. Predictable."

He had something, I thought. In that sense, life is also simple and predictable: we are born and we die. Then why do so many people read mysteries? Why do I read them?

Obviously, because I enjoy them. But why mysteries rather than some other form of fiction? I don't have to go searching for that answer: Something happens in a mystery. It has excitement, action, suspense. Unlike some so-called mainstream fiction, which after five hundred pages leaves you right back where you started, or worse, with a crisis that is never resolved, a mystery has a beginning, a middle, and an end. A reader who picks up a mystery is guaranteed a story. *Guaranteed.*

Order in life and fiction

Ah, but *Life* is not neat, comes the reply. *Life* does not resolve all problems with the loose ends neatly tied. Really? Though it may take a long time, it has been my experience that things do even out in the end. But whether or not the mystery presents an order that is artificial, it is order. It is plot.

Mysteries come in many varieties: genres within the genre. There are spy stories, psychological suspense, chases, whodunits, police procedurals, gothics. Every one of them has a strong story line, and every one is rooted in its time. For me, the really good mystery plot is as much related to its time frame as that of a good historical novel or, for that matter, as our own lives. Consider how you live now as compared to, say, ten years ago. Everything costs more, and that is restrictive. How about social conditions? If you haven't been a victim of random crime, someone in your family or close to you almost certainly has been. How does that make you feel about the police? Are you still confident that they can protect you? Many Americans are not. According to the latest statistics, a handgun is sold every thirteen seconds in the United States.

The police attitude has changed. The workload is overwhelming, and of necessity the police have adopted their own version of battlefield triage. That they have lost the public's respect—rightly or wrongly—is something else. It is the public's perception of the police and the police's perception of themselves that is important. Now, we've slipped into characterization.

But stay with plot a little longer. We've related the plot of a mystery to its time; now, let's add place. What would the plots of the Sherlock Holmes stories be without the ambience of Baker Street, hansom cabs, assassins who stalk their victims in the fog, opium dens? Life in an English country village, as portrayed by Agatha Christie, is intrinsic to Miss Marple's cases, and she relies on it for her solutions. The gritty locales of Ed McBain's fictional 87th Precinct determine the types of cases that Steve Carella and his buddies handle. The very real city of Stockholm, its permissive social code, its grim suicide wagons, are as intrinsic to Sjöwall and Wahlöö's novels as the puzzles Martin Beck struggles to solve. A more recent and most welcome addition to the ranks, Chief Inspector Arkady Renko (in Martin Cruz Smith's *Gorky Park*), of the Russian Military Police, is controlled by place as by no other factor. Even when he leaves Moscow, the force of his native land travels with him.

Consciously and subconsciously, I find that my own plots respond to changed times and conditions. The principal character of my police procedural series, Norah Mulcahaney, has become more complex in the eight years since I introduced her in *The Phone Calls,* largely in response to the stress of the city in which she works. Norah was an idealistic rookie, a member of the Women's Pool. With the liberalization of the P.D. toward women, she was able to make detective. Now she's a sergeant, and in her adventures in *The Children's Zoo,* Norah has to deal with the violent crimes of children. A few years ago, juvenile offenses were largely limited to truancy and petty theft. But more recently, in New York, a nine-year-old boy was tried for bank robbery, and a thirteen-year-old was arrested for the murder of his classmate. Norah is older, of course. She has become pragmatic, though she'll never be an opportunist. The scales are off her eyes. She no longer sees her job and the department in an idealistic glow. She's aware of the corruption on the police force, and what's worse, from her point of view—the apathy. She knows that it's caused by decaying moral values, the destruction of soul as well as body by drugs, the old people's fear of the young, the sociopathic children. The times affect how Norah feels and therefore what she does.

So, in spite of ourselves, we're back to character.

The cast of characters

Naturally, a story has to have characters. In a mystery there's the perpetrator, the victim, and the detective. Minimum. Before we go any farther, to the suspects and the pretty heroine who keeps getting into trouble by leaving her room in the middle of the night to creep downstairs and explore strange noises, think about motive. Motive is certainly part of plot. At the same time, the motive for the killing of one human being by another is based on the character of each. A rich man may be killed because he wouldn't part with his money—he's stingy; the nephew who kills him may do it because he's too lazy to work for a living. Even in the current dreadful tide of so-called motiveless murders, the character of the perpetrator is, in fact, the motive. The character of the killer also determines how he will commit the crime. I know that I'm being simplistic, but I want to stress how basic character is to plot. Character creates plot. Plot affects character. As the song says, "You can't have one without the other."

So the question comes down to this: In the mystery, how far do you go in delineating character?

My answer is—as deeply as you know how.

Having written five books in the Norah Mulcahaney series, I felt that I wanted a change of pace. Instead of a police procedural, I wanted to do a straight detective story, a puzzle. For starters I needed a new central character. Maybe a man? My editor thought I should stick with a female heroine. Fine. I was comfortable writing about a woman, but I was also afraid. By this time, Norah Mulcahaney was so familiar; she was in many ways an extension of myself, and I was worried that I might unintentionally graft some of her qualities onto my new heroine. "But," my editor pointed out, "she's not Norah, is she? She's different. Make her different." Easier said than done.

I began by doing for Mici Anhalt (a typical Hungarian name) what I had done for Norah and what I do for every character, major or minor, even if he or she appears only for half a page— a complete physical and background workup. The plot naturally dictates what kind of person he'll be—good or bad, helpful in the investigation or an impediment—but the rest I dredge up from my own observation and instinct. Physical description, age, family life, schooling, hobbies, job, emotional fulfillment or deprivation—it all goes down on paper. Maybe it never appears in the book, but it makes the character real for me. If I don't have a clear vision of him, what can I hope to pass on to the reader?

Clue: If I have to go back into the early pages of a first draft to find out a character's name, that character is not real.

Of necessity, both Mici and Norah would have to share certain qualities, certain strengths. Like Norah, Mici would have integrity, courage, self-reliance, compassion. Mici would be as efficient as Norah is—I have no patience with helpless females. So, I told myself, concentrate on the differences. Thus, Mici became physically the opposite of Norah. Where Norah is tall, dark haired, somewhat stolid, Mici is a brilliant redhead, once a professional ballet dancer, full of bounce. Mici comes from well-to-do parents. She's unmarried and has no desire to tie herself down. She doesn't sleep around, but she's not as morally rigid as Norah. (Younger, she's a product of her time.) As an investigator for the Crime Victims Compensation Board, Mici Anhalt is not a cop. She doesn't carry a gun. She can afford to bend the rules, and she does. Still, when my agent read *Aftershock,* her comment was, "She sounds like Norah with red hair."

I was sick. Where had I gone wrong? How much would I have to throw out? How much would I have to redo? Could I salvage any of it? I went back over the manuscript and told myself, she is another person; she is. Why do I see it and not the reader? And I discovered that different though Mici Anhalt most certainly was, because she felt the same emotions as Norah Mulcahaney I had superimposed Norah's reactions on her. Once I liberated Mici and let her be her own cheerful, sometimes flip and even tart self, she emerged as an individual.

Early on in the Norah Mulcahaney series, my editor complained that Norah seemed unprepared for certain situations, that she was undergoing "on-the-job training." It was true. There is no crash course for newly appointed detectives on the NYPD; they learn from experience.

The mystery story is, first and foremost entertainment. *It's got to be fun.* But it can be more, and why shouldn't it be? If character and plot interlock, it will be more rewarding for you as the writer and for your readers.

21 IT'S THE POLICE, *NOT* THE PROCEDURE

by *Gerald Petievich*

FORGET YOUR worries about what you don't know about police procedure. The appeal of the police procedural novel has little to do with actual police procedure. If readers were interested in procedure, police science textbooks would sell as well as mystery novels.

The reader who continues to turn the pages of his police story as he hangs onto a strap in the middle of a crowded bus does so *not* because of fingerprints, ballistic evidence, or plaster casts of footprints. Jerking along from stop to stop, he reads because he is enthralled. It's regular guys like him versus child murderers, hired killers, heroin pushers. He is mesmerized by the bottom line of literature: human behavior.

The reader must be able to identify with the cops and the crooks in your book. I believe this identification is critical. The police procedural is a story of man against the odds, a tale of alienation. The detective is not just a visitor to the world of evil. He, and his villains, are residents. Their behavior should be believable without being trite; surprising, but within the realm of the reader's imagination. The writer's job is to provide footholds for the reader to keep him from getting confused, or worse, bored on the trip through the underworld.

What kinds of characters will be interesting enough to keep the man on the bus reading your book? Let's start with the crooks: To find out about them go to the police station. There, don't expect to have all your questions about the bad guys answered. You could spend years hanging around the detective bureau, and you'd still be waiting to hear the bulls throw out any theories of why crooks do the things they do. You'd be lucky to get a policeman even to venture a guess. Why? Because they just plain don't know. They haven't the slightest idea. Neither do sociologists, judges, parole officials, or psychologists. Of course *they* will be more than happy to venture a guess; they are the ones who write books about criminal behavior. As a fiction writer, keep away from such books lest dogma infect your manuscript.

Observe, don't analyze

You are a writer. A painter of people. All you need to know to be able to write a police procedural is *how* criminals act; forget *why*. To learn how they act, listen to the stories you hear at the police station and take good notes: pliers marks on the bodies of children; a confidence man who impersonates a bank examiner in order to steal from the elderly; a bank robber who wears a suit and tie and drives a shiny Cadillac for a getaway car. These are the things policemen know about. It is the conflict and emotion implicit in such stories on which readers will judge you.

If you're still having second doubts about how to create a believable bad guy, I suggest you use people you know. Erase most or all of your best friend's conscience, and on paper he or she would probably be a very convincing crook.

Beware of embellishing your crook's character with a lot of thought narration. The criminal's viewpoint is a danger area for the writer. Though I occasionally violate this rule in my books, narratives based on such a restricted and unsympathetic viewpoint usually are perilous. This is not to say that the reader needs to *like* the crook. On the contrary, you should hope that he will hate the crook. The point is that the reader must be able to *identify* with the crooks as well as with the cops. All your characters must be drawn so that there is no mistaking the fact that, crooks or not, they were born, raised, and had a part in the grammar school Thanksgiving play. Bad guys are not Martians.

Believable motives

Another pitfall is the tendency of the writer to attribute a crook's behavior to bizarre motives. This is an easy trap to fall into; because you have a conscience, you assume that anyone who robs a bank, besides needing the money, must be under some sort of psychological pressure. Well, the reader doesn't want your fantasy explanation for the robber's lifestyle, any more than the cop on the beat wants to be told that crooks are all victims of socio-economic deprivation. The reader has his own ideas as to what causes crime. If your character can stir his imagination, you will be able to get your point of view across without sounding like an attorney.

To get around the danger of creating shopworn, one-dimensional characters, just show the bank robber getting dressed in his suit and tie, driving to the bank, robbing it, and speeding off in his new Cadillac. Not only will the reader understand exactly what happened at the bank, he'll be able to tell you lots about the robber. You will have flicked on his mind's fantasy switch. The general rule is, *let the bad guy's character be shown by his actions.*

My advice on how to draw your policemen or detectives is the same: let action speak. Thought narration by the detective is not as dangerous as by the crook (although it's an easy way for a reader to get bored). In fact, this is an area in your novel in which you can do a little improvising. The detective's thoughts will probably be close to your own. And so be it. Since policemen are not all aggressive, dynamic, good at remembering details, patient, clean-cut, or right-wing, but rather pretty much like you and everyone else, you will have created a believable character.

There are two qualities your policeman or detective must have to make him believable and sympathetic. First, he must *care*. The more personal his involvement in the case the better. No one is interested in reading about an investigation of a crime from a neutral viewpoint. This is where you can be most creative. Go ahead. Let your detective fall in love with the victim's sister.

Second, the detective must act with authority. I don't mean his badge. I mean ability to recognize (not necessarily understand) the evil he sees and accept it as medical doctors do cancer. They diagnose it and deal with it. Detectives are not shocked by the horrors of crime, after their first couple of weeks on the job. From then on, for most cops it's just sort of an underlying hostility. Policemen handle these feelings in different ways, but they do *handle* them: they repress them. You can imagine how you would feel arresting a murderer who was on parole for murder.

Asking the right questions

The only police procedure you need to know about in order to write your novel is asking questions. This is the police procedure that solves ninety percent of all crimes: talking to people—witnesses, informants, crooks, victims. Real detectives solve crimes the same way a lost vacationer finds the Holiday Inn in a strange town. He asks. People give directions. Sometimes the directions are right. Sometimes the directions are wrong. Almost all cases are solved in just this way.

I am not saying that cops don't use fingerprints and computers. But as any good detective will tell you, the crime computer is only as good as the information in it. It does not know who the culprit is, and fingerprints are only useful if you have some fingers with which to compare them.

Keep in mind that the man reading on the bus is already an expert in police work. If he doesn't have a doctorate—as most of us do not—he at least has his B. A. in gumshoeing from the University of TV and Movies. You should treat him like the expert that he is. Besides, there is no police procedure, no investigative tool, that can be as interesting as a few good lines of action or dialogue from even the most colorless of human beings.

Cop talk? You can pick up enough during one visit to the squad room to carry you through any police procedural. And don't be inhibited by your doubts as to whether your detective's language would be accepted by the most hard-boiled dick in Brooklyn. If the characters are right, even he will like your book.

For the reader, it's the conflicts, the challenges, the successes and failures in the policeman's world of alienation and sorrow that will raise his emotions. It's the people, not the procedure.

22 WHAT WILL HAPPEN— AND WHEN?

by *Richard Martin Stern*

WHAT IS there to say about suspense in fiction? That it belongs in whodunits and the cliff-hangers of adventure tales, and has no place in "straight, serious" fiction? Poppycock.

Suspense in its broadest form is the stuff of which all fiction is, or ought to be made. It is suspense that catches the reader's interest, carries him along with you, makes him turn the page and read on instead of putting the book down for—maybe— another time. Think about it.

Would you go back into the theatre for the last act of, say, *Hamlet,* if the author had not with conscious craft led you to the point where you simply had to know what was going to happen and how? And isn't that what suspense is all about?

I have read that people lined the wharf in New York waiting for the mail packet from England to dock so they could read the latest installment of Dickens's *Old Curiosity Shop* to find out if Little Nell did indeed die. If that is not suspense, I don't know the meaning of the word.

But how does the writer manage to achieve it?

Ah, there we get to the heart of the matter. I do not pretend that I have any formula for instant success, but there are certain guidelines that can be set forth.

Guidelines

First and foremost, the reader must care. That sounds obvious; unfortunately too many writers forget it. The reader must care, and that means that he must have an interest in the characters. Plot alone will not do it.

People are born, fall in love, grow sick and die every day, but you don't know them and so what happens to them is not really important to you. But when these things happen to someone close, someone you care about, then these events are drama, and you await their outcome in a mood that can only be called suspenseful.

How many stories or books have you and I started to read and then tossed aside because we didn't give a damn what happened to the names that appeared on the pages? All manner of weird and wonderful things could be going on, but unless the writer had given us characters with whom we could identify and about whom we cared, there was no urge to turn the page; there was no quality of suspense.

In remarks he made at West Point, William Faulkner kept returning to a single phrase: "the human heart in conflict." Another way to put it is with the question my agent used to ask too often about stories of mine: "Where is the love versus duty?" A phrase and a question that go directly to character, which is where it all begins.

That is not to say that plot is unimportant in the building of suspense. Plot is very important, obviously, because without it nothing happens—as is the case in what I refer to as "navel novels," where everyone sits around cross-legged contemplating his identity crisis—and what is suspenseful about that?

And so characters there must be about whom the reader cares, and plot to provide action and to demonstrate the human heart in conflict—and quite probably love versus duty. Now you have the tools with which to build suspense. How do you go about it?

Well, one way you do *not* go about it is by trickery. Dishonesty will out and become in the current jargon "counterproductive." As a writer friend of mine puts it, if your character opens a can of beans, somebody has to eat them. You can do all manner of things to misdirect your reader, as a magician onstage misdirects your attention, but the rabbit you eventually pull out of the hat has to be a real rabbit, not a mouse you sneaked in at the last moment as a substitute. Level with your reader, and he will go along; cheat him and you have lost your audience. So much for the *do nots*.

A sense of time

In many, if not most, stories, a sense of time is important, and this can be a powerful tool with which to build suspense. The minutes, the hours, the days are ticking away, and will whatever is going to happen take place in time? Turn the pages and see. In my long novel, *The Tower,* the entire action takes place in less than twelve hours, and the major action in a little over four. For purposes of plot (suspense) it was mandatory that the ticking minutes be emphasized. I used the simple device, by no means original, of heading each chapter with its time span, thereby making time itself a part of the story. Thus: 9:00 a.m.—9:33 a.m.; 11:10 a.m.—12:14 p.m.; etc. The final paragraph reads: "The time was 8:41. It had been four hours and eighteen minutes since the explosion." I have been told that the device was successful.

Sequence is another factor that is important in the building of suspense. Again, that ought to be obvious, but I am afraid it not always is. How many books or stories have you and I read in which the writer has shot the works halfway through his tale, and from that point on it is plodding downhill? Where then has suspense gone?

Sometimes I like to think of a story as a kind of hill climb. You start at the bottom and work your way up. There are dips and rises, but always you are working toward the top of the hill. When you arrive at the top, which is the story's climax, you face a steep drop-off, and you get to the bottom just as quickly as you can. Why? Because you have used up your suspense, you have shot the works, you have sung your big aria, and, to continue to mix the figures of speech, you want to get offstage while the audience is still applauding.

Pace and climax

A writer friend of mine once asked, "Where do you go when you've started your story on high C?" Good question, and I think the answer is that you drop an octave or two as fast as you can and then start climbing again. You want your story to build, its pace to quicken, its excitement to grow— then you are building the suspense and pulling the reader along with you.

Do not mistake me. The growth can be quiet, understated, low-key; C. P. Snow's novels come to mind, or Marquand's. But the growth, the quickening pace, the climb to the top of the hill ought to be there, and in Snow's and Marquand's novels it is; and so is suspense. C. P. Snow spoke of the "narrative art," and when he was asked what he meant, he said that it is the art of making the reader turn the page. Is that not precisely what we are talking about?

In the heyday of the great national magazines, the "slicks," the craft of serial writing reached a high state of expertise. Basically, the serial was a single story running through, let us say, three installments of thirty pages each. (There could be as few as two installments, or as many as eight, but the technical problems remained the same.) Each installment had to carry on the main story, but it also had to have a smaller story of its own, a subplot, if you will, or at least a large problem presented but not completely solved, thereby whetting the reader's appetite for the next issue in which problem number one would be solved, and problem number two presented. And so it went, the story rising in pitch to the final installment in which everything was solved and the story quickly ended.

It is, I think, not a bad format to keep in mind. Probably because I served my apprenticeship in the slicks, I find it ingrained in my subconscious. Always the story must rise—but not too fast. As with a pot that must not be allowed to boil over, the heat must be reduced, slowed down, to let the reader take a few easy breaths and maybe go out to the refrigerator for a fresh beer. Then start at him again, making the story rise, quicken, so that tension mounts. This is the essence, and whether you are writing mystery, adventure, romance, "straight, serious" fiction, or whatever, juveniles or adults, hardcover or soft, this is the way to C. P. Snow's "narrative art," the art of making the reader turn the page. This is suspense.

23 SETTING AND BACKGROUND IN THE NOVEL

by *Mary Stewart*

ALTHOUGH I must confess that I have my doubts whether one writer can tell another how to write anything at all, or even describe adequately how he does it himself, I know that there is something heartening and helpful about the very community of experience. Every writer started somewhere, and no writer worth his salt ever had it easy, or ever will; so it is possible that a brief attempt to summarize the way I tackle certain phases of writing may be of interest to others.

Place makes plot

Almost without my realizing it, I have come to have the reputation of setting my suspense stories exotically—Avignon, Skye, Savoy, Corfu—and of using these settings not just as background color, but dynamically, almost as a "first character" of the book. I do, in fact, start with the setting. I used to think it was chance that led me into this way of writing. When I wrote my first book, *Madam, Will You Talk?*, I had never written a story before, and it seemed natural, in that icy winter when the impulsion to write finally outweighed even my diffidence in starting, to choose the most exciting—and the hottest—place I had then been to. I found, in the writing of the book, that the tough, strange, romantic setting exactly suited the kind of thing I wanted to write; that it did, in fact, dictate its own kind of plot; and that to allow it to permeate every corner of the story could do nothing but enrich that story.

This was obviously the kind of thing that suited me, so, book by book, from this kind of start I formed my own personal work map. A place which had had a powerful impact on my senses and imagination would suggest a story line and an atmosphere into which I could put my characters, and let their reactions to the setting, and to each other in that setting, work themselves out into a plot. The fact that I chose a different setting for each of my books made (I think) for variety in treatment and atmosphere, even though the basic ingredients of the "suspense novel" must to some extent stay the same.

Of course I did not discover this working method by chance, as, in fact, each writer's way of working must come out of deep-rooted patterns of thought and behavior which at some point find their own way of expression. I can see now where my own method came from. I am country bred, with a deep interest in natural history, over which is grafted my profession of English Literature, and a passion for ancient history and folk-lore. So I find that my type of imagination quickens most readily in beautiful places where legend and history add an extra light of excitement to the kind of life that is lived there today.

This work map, like all writers' methods, is an intensely personal thing, and, while it suits me, it would possibly suit nobody else; but my own use of setting as a take-off point, and thereafter as an integral part of the novel, has suggested to me one or two general observations which may possibly be of interest or use.

Dynamic and static uses of place

I suppose there are two main uses of setting, the dynamic and the static. Probably the best example of the former—

where the place is as vivid as the people—is Emily Brontë's *Wuthering Heights*. In this, the prototype of the romantic novel, the characters grow out of the place, and so does the action; the story would be unthinkable in any other setting. Wuthering Heights itself is the hero, not Heathcliff, who is in a way only a humanization of the stormy moorland and is most "real" when he is a voice in the wind.

What I have called static setting is more common; that is, the use of setting merely as a background for human action, the giving of a local habitation and a name to a story which could have happened almost anywhere.

Whichever way the setting is used, it is of paramount importance. I have, in the past, come across novels with scanty or token settings, in which the people moved and talked against no vividly defined background. Of these novels I can now remember nothing except the growing exasperation and difficulty of reading, which I at length traced to its cause. On the other hand, novels which were trivial apart from their vivid settings, for example, the stories of Gene Stratton Porter, have remained in my mind ever since my teens when I read them.

Any attempt to set a novel vividly and dynamically must involve descriptive writing. This is a real danger point, and should be done with care, and sparely. The "set piece" describing a place is by its nature static, and should be used only where action needs to be temporarily suspended, like the pause in music. It should never be used for its own sake, and it should not be used at length. But the periodic interruption of the action by brief descriptive passages can be a powerful weapon in the writer's hand. These can work like the curtain in the theatre—to open a scene, or act as changeover points for emphasis and direction either of action or emotion. They can break up a long dialogue or action sequence and provide points of rest; they can be emotive; they can also allow the writer to slip essential information in among semi-relevant or purely atmospheric detail.

Sensation by action

Most important of all, perhaps, is the power that a vivid setting gives you, the writer, over your reader: the way it lets you catapult him bodily into the action. Nothing takes a reader more immediately into the being of a fictional character than the swift recognition of some common experience: "Yes, it does feel like that . . . or smell like that . . . or look like that." By exploiting the simple sensation, the writer can transport his reader into the character's skin, transcending barriers of personality, even of sex. The quickest and most vivid way is the concrete one, that is, not the abstract description of sensation, but the illustration of sensation by action. Once the action has suggested the sensation to the reader, once you can get him vividly to share the physical responses of the character, he is also free to enter that character's mind.

To take a random example from a book of mine, *My Brother Michael*: There is a point where the heroine, herself in considerable danger, is forced to be a silent witness to a particularly unpleasant murder.

> I shut my eyes. I turned my head away so that my cheek, like my hands, pressed against the cool rock. It smelt fresh, like rain. I remember that under my left hand there was a little knob of stone the shape of a limpet shell.

Later:

> I was shaking, and covered with sweat, and hot as though the chilly cleft were an oven. Under the fingers of my left hand the stone limpet had broken away, and it was embedded in the flesh, hurting me. . . .

Two things have been done here. The feel and smell of damp rock, which everyone recognizes, have taken the reader inside the girl's skin and therefore right into her predicament; and her unconscious action in breaking off the bit of stone should suggest stress of mind more vividly than any direct statement. It is a fact that in moments of severe stress, one's mind often fastens on some small physical irrelevancy which may remain in the memory more vividly even than the agony itself.

(I would suggest here in passing that the dynamic use of setting is a weapon that no historical novelist can afford to ignore. To describe scenes, dresses, ways of life of a different age, may make the story move like a pageant in front of us; but to take us alive into another period of time, the senses must be invoked in the way described above. This was the challenge that I took up when I wrote my first historical novel *The Crystal Cave*. It was not deliberate choice that gave me as my setting the most obscure period of British history, the "dark age." It might be argued that this freed the imagination more than a better-known period, but it did involve building a "real" and plausible world out of something unknown and unmapped and, moreover, obscured further beneath a veil of implausible tradition. I used the same resources and techniques as in my suspense novels: community of experience laid over careful research. People think differently in different times, but their bodies feel and react as they always did. The animal is older than the human spirit.)

Vivid close-ups

As for the actual techniques of description and setting, here, as everywhere, the basic rule is simplicity. The most vivid "atmospheric" setting is done, not with elaborate description which tires the reader's powers of mental build-up, but with the selection of one or two telling details. This is how Graham Greene, one of the masters of setting, does it. No long, drawn-out panning down the village street, just one short, vivid close-up of a vulture hunched on a corrugated iron roof in tropical rain, and you have all the torrid squalor of Africa in a sentence. And this same detail occurs again. The repetition is effective and cumulative, but needs a practiced hand, or the device edges toward symbolism, which is a clumsy way of "getting through," and ineffective when the symbolism is the personal symbolism of the author, and not the real thing worn smooth with—literally—centuries of use. A good story should be carried alive into the heart of the reader, and this is only done by the writer's passion disciplined by the writer's skill in the techniques of communication.

Every writer finds his own techniques, but perhaps I could suggest one or two ideas which were starting points for me. In the description of a whole landscape, a wide-angle picture, it is probably best to start at the horizon and work in. Draw in from the large general effects of sky and atmosphere, till you get to the close-ups, the plants at the edge of the road where your observer is standing. Of course, there are times when you must do it the other way around, but choose which way to direct the observer's eye, and keep to it.

A physical setting should never be built up too elaborately. What a writer is doing is opening a gateway on *someone else's imagination.* You have to build your effects by using the reader's experience and terms of reference at the same time as your own. So don't force his imagination too hard into the shape of yours. Give him the main points, place them for him, and then let him fill in out of his own experience. He'll do this anyway, so there is no point in distorting his picture with yours. For example, nothing is worse than reading a detailed description of a room. Something of the size and style and color, and perhaps three telling details, are all that is necessary. If the reader furnishes the room with pieces he knows, it will be all the more vivid for him. I, myself, always found illustrated books very trying; they clashed with my own much more (to me) vivid picture.

And now let me finish with an apology. First of all, for using my own work as an illustration; but the only writer of whose motives you are almost sure is yourself, and motive, rather than result, was what concerned me. Second, for having certainly done, almost everywhere in my own writing, the exact opposite of what I have suggested here. But there are, I repeat, no rules. And I am well aware that no writer who is worth anything ever writes to anyone else's plan. All he does is to read what the other fellow says, raise an eyebrow, mutter "I couldn't work like that," and go his own way.

24 ENGAGING THE EMOTIONS OF YOUR READER

by *Dorothy Uhnak*

RECENTLY, I was introduced to a woman who surprised me by her familiarity with the characters in my novel, *The Investigation.* She had read it when it was published—a few years ago—and assured me that she had read many books since then. And yet, she recalled things about my characters that I had forgotten. "How did you make them so real?" she asked me. "How did you keep *me* caring, not just as I read the book but even now?"

Aside from being very flattering, her question, from a writer's point of view, is very basic and very important. How do we take words and turn them into people our readers will come to regard as living, feeling, breathing, fellow human beings? How do we engage our readers' emotions so they care enough to turn the page, and then the next, right to the very end?

When I was writing *The Investigation,* I got off to a very bad start. The novel, in part, tells about a beautiful, enigmatic young woman who is accused of murdering her two children. Taking the narrator's point of view, I had the woman come across as somewhat less than human: My dislike of my main character, the narrator, stopped the book cold. There was nowhere to go except back to a new beginning.

A small voice kept asking, what is she really like? Beneath the veneer, the aggressive self-control and polish, who is this tough-talking, steely-eyed woman? The questioning voice grew into the male protagonist, Joe Peters, and the story was told, first-person, by Joe. He was a world-weary, seen-everything, fifty-year-old cop with his own life history, his own problems, his own experience and expertise. Through his surprisingly compassionate eyes, I began to seek out the human factor, the hint of *vulnerability* which would connect Kitty Keeler to the rest of humanity and separate her from the crime of which she was accused.

In my earlier novels, Christie Opara, the detective/heroine of my trilogy* about the only young woman in an otherwise all-male District Attorney's Squad, could easily have become an unpleasant character. As she presented herself, Christie seemed opinionated, stubborn, self-righteous, unbending in her standards of right and wrong. However, seen through the eyes of her boss, District Attorney Casey Reardon, she became not tough or hard, but rather, strong and protective; not so much puritanically rigid as idealistic, sensitive, and caring of other people. She set high standards not only for herself, but for others. She found it difficult to accept less than the best in people.

In the course of the trilogy, instances of Christie's courage and quick thinking and integrity were often offset by allowing a glimpse of her fear, her uncertainty, her discomfit at the realization that life is not made up of absolutes. The reader was made aware of Christie's human *vulnerability*.

Linking characters to readers

A key to the humanness of my characters, to their reality, lies in that word: *vulnerability*. It is the link that reaches out to

---

*The trilogy includes *The Bait, The Witness,* and *The Ledger.*

the reader: No matter how strange, remote, unknown, foreign, esoteric, intriguing a character might be, I try to give my reader a sense of recognition. Even as you and I, this person is vulnerable in certain situations and moments. Having worked for fourteen years as a detective in New York City, I write of the world that I have inhabited intimately. I realize that for most people, this is largely a fictional world that they need to be introduced into carefully. As a police officer, with all the marvelous, unprecedented opportunities for a writer to learn about human behavior, I constantly sought to look beneath the surface of the people around me. Whether acting with my fellow officers or dealing with criminals or with complainants, or with victims or victimizers; whether hearing accusations or excuses, lies or truths, my mind searched automatically for the vulnerability of a world-toughened partner or a dreadfully repugnant, nearly subhuman rapist. How does he connect with me, with my thoughts, my feelings, my life, my humanity? I might not like the person—indeed, police work puts one constantly in touch with very unlikable, despicable characters.

Exploring the vulnerability of a character does not necessarily make him more sympathetic to the reader. Quite the contrary, in some cases. We may be able to accept—intellectually, at any rate—the psychopath who operates from a rationality of his own, a person to whom life is not sacred, to whom any means justifies his personal ends. I presented an arch villain in the *The Investigation* in the person of an old, dying, very evil Mafioso don. He is shown in all his human vulnerability: flesh as our flesh, pain as our pain. And yet, on his deathbed, he makes jokes about the fact that yes, he can admit now he was responsible for the death by explosion of a son-in-law who displeased him. Yes, he felt a little sorry for the young woman blown up with the son-in-law when the rigged car shattered their lives. But—and here is his vulnerability—he is frantic over the detective's threat to reveal a secret to the old man's daughter. The secret would cause his daughter to dishonor his memory; that thought is intolerable, unbearable. After all, he loves and cherishes his daughter beyond all things, and her approval and love have been essential to him.

Thus we see that we cannot explain this man as an aberration, as a psychopath incapable of human feeling. He is far worse; he is *human;* he *does* have feelings, even as you and I. He does understand fear and suffering; he just doesn't care when other people are concerned if his self-interests are involved.

Probing for the weak spot

No sane person considers himself "despicable." Clever, sharp, shrewd, aware, "taking care of number one"—sure. But *despicable*? That is another person's judgment. In zeroing in on a character, in order to make valid the judgment made by another character, I find it essential to decribe not only what he looks like, sounds like, how he moves, how he sees other people, how they see him; I also try to dig into the center of the character, to find his point of sensitivity, no matter how minute it might be. To find the vulnerable moment whereby he might reveal himself, for good or ill.

It is essential for writers to *care* about the characters they create. How many times do we read a story or novel and after a few pages find ourselves backtracking—who is this man? how was he described earlier? was he the brother or the lover or what? A sense of ambiguity on the part of the writer leads to feelings of frustration on the part of the reader. After all, if the writer doesn't care enough about a character, why should the reader?

My way of caring, of bringing the reader emotionally into the story, is to touch on the humanity of my characters. By being made to care about the characters, the reader moves along with the story, turns those pages and, we hope, waits for our next work.

25
THE IMPORTANCE OF BEING PLAUSIBLE
by *Michael Underwood*

ALTHOUGH PUBLISHERS on both sides of the Atlantic may be facing economic difficulties, the mystery novel is as buoyant and thriving as ever. I believe that the intelligent and well-written mystery will continue to find a place on publishers' lists, thanks to the enduring loyalty of mystery readers as a class, many of whom can be properly described as addicts.

In reading a recent issue of *Current Crime* (a British quarterly review of mysteries "worth reading"), I was struck by seeing so many familiar and well-known mystery writers' names, names of practitioners whose novels have been published regularly over several decades. This is very heartening to someone like me, who both writes and reads mysteries. Indeed, I began reading them long before I ever tried to write one, and I'm now into my fourth decade of being published.

I spoke of the survival of the intelligent and well-written mystery, for if any category suffered from the economic recession, it is the mechanically written story with its contrived plot and its implausible happenings, the sort of book in which bloodshed and violent physical action are a substitute for more durable virtues. Not all of us, of course, can write with the style and grace of, say, Graham Greene, or create the crackling dialogue of Raymond Chandler, or plot with the ingenuity of Agatha Christie, but it's still possible to write a book in lucid English. The great majority of mystery writers not only achieve this basic requirement, but manage to add their own hallmarks in felicity of expression.

Whatever sort of crime story you choose to write, remember that the plot is of paramount importance. Plots come more easily to some than others. I am one of those writers who finds the construction of a plot akin to chipping away at solid rock with a toothpick. I look with envy—and also with a certain measure of suspicion—at fellow writers who tell me they have so many plots in their heads that they will never live long enough to use them.

However substantial your other writing skills, I venture to say that, unless you have a sound plot, you will not write a good crime story. You may feel you can get by with an absorbing background and interesting characters, but if the plot is deficient, this will eventually become apparent; the reader will experience a sense of letdown by the time he reaches the end of your book. Indeed, the greater the writer's *other* skills, the greater the reader's sense of letdown if the plot is weak, as the reader will have been carried forward, expecting a satisfying denouement, and then be deprived of this at the very last moment. I always know when I have a good plot, i.e. a natural plot, and I am ruefully aware when I have a contrived plot.

And the book with the contrived or artificial plot is a much harder one to write.

For me, a contrived plot relies on coincidence and fortuitous happenings. A natural one is one in which nothing jars or stretches credulity but leaves the reader utterly satisfied at the end. It all fits together like a well-made jigsaw; nothing has to be forced into place.

Jarring details

Given, then, that the present-day mystery writer meets these various demands and also manages to give his books interesting and colorful backgrounds, what one defect so often detracts from complete reader satisfaction?

In my view, it is lack of plausibility—not plausibility of the story as a whole, because if that is lacking, the book is fatally flawed, but plausibility of a part. Have we not all read mysteries that absorbed our interest and swept us deliciously along until, suddenly, we are jarred by an implausibility of some sort? It may be a character who behaves out of pattern for the sake of a plot (a contrivance, in fact), or a piece of action that doesn't ring true.

As a writer, I'm aware of having transgressed in this respect, usually when the plot itself has a defect or hasn't been sufficiently thought out.

To give an example of what I mean, I recall reading an excellent thriller set behind the Iron Curtain, in which much of the action was taken up with the hero's eluding and eventually escaping from the clutches of the country's security police. There was a cliff-hangingly exciting climax before he was able to get out of the country. But in the final chapter he returned there on a commercial flight, blithely going through the customs and immigration procedure he had so recently managed to outwit in the course of an illegal escape. This, to me, was a jarring implausibility in an otherwise first-rate novel.

Today's readers demand more than a mere puzzle. Having constructed your plot, you must not allow yourself to be deflected from it. In a crime novel, nothing should happen that is not relevant to the plot. You may be brilliant at baking bread and long to share your expertise with your readers. You should do so, however, only if the loaf you have lovingly described baking in chapter 4 is going to poison the victim in chapter 7, or become the conveyor of a time bomb to be placed on his breakfast table in chapter 10. Nothing, repeat, nothing, should appear in your book which does not further the plot. The plot is everything. You may be able to get away with a deficiency of plot in other forms of fiction, but not in a crime novel.

What can be done about these often small, but deadly, implausibilities? Cosmetic surgery is usually the answer. Frequently no more than a couple of sentences or a paragraph are needed to rectify the flaw. The more experienced the writer, the more artful and expert his surgery. For example, suppose you have a character who has been depicted as having a morbid phobia about water; you can't have him suddenly jump into a river, even to save a child from drowning, without having first prepared the reader for such an about-face. I wouldn't think, however, it would take many words to persuade your reader that your character's action was perfectly plausible in the given circumstances. It merely means taking a bit more trouble with the scene in question so that it doesn't strain the reader's credibility.

Sometimes, of course, what is or is not plausible is largely a matter of opinion, and then a writer can either argue for his own viewpoint or submit to another's. As a writer who has also been a lawyer, I'm reasonably good at arguing my own case, though often there's no case to argue when one accepts the validity of another view—for example, that of one's editor.

Some thirty years ago, a publisher's reader remarked of my first book that it had obviously been written by a woman (which I am not) who was at home in the kitchen (which I am), but who was miles out of her depth when it came to describing court and police procedure. At the time I was working in the Public Prosecutor's Department in London, so whatever other faults the book had (and they were many), it was totally authentic in the depiction of its police and court scenes. Was the reader an ass or had I failed, despite my firsthand knowledge, to make those scenes plausible? Modesty should probably compel me to admit the latter, but I think the answer was that the reader had been so saturated with the unauthentic that he was unable to recognize the real thing when it came along.

Strong plots, credible endings

The sort of implausibilities I have been talking about are more likely to be found in the final chapters of a book when all the ends are being tied up. If the reader is to close the book with that feeling of total satisfaction that the writer must always strive for, the ending has to be right. My own belief is that the sounder the plot, the smoother the ending and the less the danger of implausibilities. When the plot is weak or contrived or ill-conceived, then the implausibilities are likely to develop and the reader will put down the book with a feeling of disappointment and, possibly, in a mood of exasperation. If it's only disappointment, he may give you another chance with your next novel. But if it's worse than that, he is less likely to do so. It is salutary for writers to reflect that few readers' loyalty is infinite. And, after all, if you don't have readers, you won't have a publisher—for long. How often one has heard friends say, "Oh, I used to read his books, but he seems to have gone off recently. . . ." It may be that their own tastes have changed and they're tired of the particular sort of story they once enjoyed. If so, it's merely a case of slings and arrows for the poor old author. But if the writer really has lost form, it's important for him to find out quickly in what way. Perhaps a certain tiredness has manifested itself in his writing, his plots (yes, plots again) are weaker, and the implausibilities in the action have become more difficult to swallow.

In one sense, it's a miracle that mystery writers are still able to dream up fresh plots, when, by rights, all the basic ones have long since been used. Of course they have been, which underlines the need to give them fresh twists and a new look. The basic motives for committing murder (gain, revenge, jealousy) can be counted on the fingers of half a hand and have been doing service for over a hundred years. But they can still be set in a fresh context. Nobody knows that better than present-day mystery writers, whose ingenuity knows no bounds. But we must all guard against those small implausibilities that can needlessly blemish our stories.

26 SPRINGBOARD TO SUSPENSE FICTION

by *Phyllis A. Whitney*

THERE IS ONE question that is always asked of the writer by the non-writer and it comes so often that those of us who write develop an automatic wince when we hear it. The question, of course, is, "Where do you get your ideas?" It's not that it isn't a legitimate question, but that the answer seems both so obvious and so complicated that it is hard to answer.

The simple, obvious answer is, "Everywhere," and it sends the questioner away as mystified as ever. Since non-writers never have any ideas for stories, there seems a magic in the way a complicated novel starts from nothing—and appears as a whole in a printed book.

It is the complicated part of that answer that I would like to deal with here. Because, of course, there are many, many times when the writer has no ideas at all, when we start from scratch and often without inspiration. We then do need a springboard to launch us into that first idea, to which other ideas will keep attaching themselves until hundreds of manuscript pages have been filled and we have that completed book.

The non-writer doesn't understand that a plot is not something that appears full-blown, miraculously, from nowhere. It is something that grows painstakingly, a bit at a time, often through periods of despair and drought. Yet there *are* mo-

161

ments when miracles do happen and something comes clear in an instant—though not as a rule the whole thing.

Pleasure in places

My own springboard, from which I take off in the beginning, is usually a new setting. I have a strong feeling toward places, and when I am entranced by a setting, I can take pleasure in writing about it as a background for my story. A real setting furnishes endless ideas for story scenes, and even gives me an introduction to people who may be helpful in working out my characters. I don't like to transfer real people into my stories, because they would never behave as I want them to. But the ideas expressed by those I talk with in a special setting give me the knowledge to make my own characters in such a setting true to life.

While the background must always come early in the development of a story for me, it is not necessarily the first springboard. A year or so ago, I had a strange dream. I don't usually remember dreams, but I woke up with this one vividly in mind. I had been wandering on a hillside, perhaps a mountainside, with woods all around. Set down in the middle of this wooded area was what appeared to be a huge, circular barn. The door was locked, but I went in anyway, as one does in dreams, to behold the strangest of scenes: a bullring, with a larger-than-life-size stone bull standing in the center of it. Mystery, with no answer, because I woke up immediately and with just one thought in mind: *What a wonderful title for a book*.

I lost the barn in the course of writing the novel, but *The Stone Bull* became the title of my next book, and I now know all about that bull on the mountainside. My setting came second in the development of this story—when I had to choose my mountain. Since the Catskills are not too far from where I live, I found a suitable area and went there to stay for a week.

Once I am in the place of my choice, I work hard every minute. I fill a notebook with random description and set down any plot ideas that may come to me, inspired by the place. I take several rolls of color film, turning my camera on anything that might be useful to me when I get home. I take advantage of everything the place offers that might give me story material—hiking trails, rowing a boat, riding in a truck —or whatever. I collect maps of the region, colored postcards, brochures, books. Sometimes my collection grows so heavy that I have to send it home separately. But I am seldom able to spend more than a week to ten days in any place I visit. Because of my "outsider's" view, I always write from the viewpoint of a stranger new to the area.

One of the most interesting and rewarding setting searches I've made was on a trip to Norway. It came about by chance. While working on one book, I always have an eye open for anything that may lead me into the next one. A friend had just returned from a trip to Scandinavia, and she spoke with enthusiasm of the colorful city of Bergen. I went to the library and looked up Bergen, and my compass direction was set for Norway.

I try, if possible, to prepare for my arrival on the new scene by writing letters ahead of time. Even when my books were not well known, I wrote to librarians before I arrived and usually found a warm welcome. I go to travel agencies, and send letters to consulates, explaining that I mean to write about a certain locality, and I am often given introductions and offers of help. Doors may sometimes be slammed suspiciously in my face, but no writer ever takes "no" for an answer, and I keep insisting that I must get off the beaten track, find out how people live, see the inside of a few homes. The tourist things are fine, but I want more than that.

On location

Once on location, I choose carefully those things to do that will be most useful to me. Bergen is a small place geographically, and was easy to cover. When I was writing about Istan-

bul, I had a more difficult problem. I couldn't possibly come
in as a stranger and learn all about that exotic city in a short
time. But I had done my homework by reading and knew that
I would visit one famous mosque, a fortress on the Bosporus,
one covered bazaar, a village on the water, and other sights.
To these I would return more than once, so that I could come
to know them well. Of course, once you are in a place, there
will be things to see and do that you couldn't dream of ahead
of time. The unexpected is always happening, and you will fit
it into your schedule if it seems to offer possibilities.

As a suspense writer, I am always alert for two things in
particular: A likely means of murder that fits the setting, and
the right place for the "chase" scene of my climax. It is sometimes disconcerting to residents when I exclaim with delight
that some spot of beauty or historic significance is a lovely
place for a murder!

In Bergen I discovered my climax setting when we drove
out to visit one of the few remaining wooden churches that
date back to the beginnings of Christianity in Norway, and
which have been marvelously preserved. This one was a
museum piece a little way out of Bergen, and its setting was
an eerie park of gnarled roots and forbidding pines. I took a
dozen pictures right there, and when I came to my climax
scene, I had details to use that I could never have captured
fully in notes alone. The pictures were so real that I could even
invoke my mood, my feelings about the place.

A character and the search

Once my setting has been chosen, there is another means of
launching me into my story that I must immediately seek. I
must develop a main character faced by a problem, and I must
find a means to get her to the setting of my choice.

In the case of *Listen for the Whisperer,* a romantic suspense
novel set in Bergen, I started out with the idea of a young

woman who had been abandoned as a child by her famous actress mother and raised by the father she adores. She has grown up resenting the entire legend of her mother, a woman who is now living in Norway, and whom she hasn't seen since birth. Her father in dying has left word that he wants her to seek out her mother. She goes there against her will, with an obligation to fulfill. Thus we are launched into a psychological situation filled with opportunities for emotion, conflict—and, of course, mystery.

Before writing *The Golden Unicorn,* I wasn't able to travel abroad, and had to choose a setting closer to hand. The village of East Hampton on Long Island was suggested to me by a writer friend, and I went out to spend a few days there. When a setting is not as foreign and exotic as I like, I must especially seek out small things. I must walk the hard sand of a beach near the water's edge, with all the summer people gone, and with a feeling of loneliness, of sadness, because winter lies ahead and the empty houses are shuttered. I must *experience* this. My own emotions must be examined for every nuance. I take snapshots of the old beach houses peering down from their high dunes. I note the scraps of broken shell, the dark seaweed cast upon empty sand, a line of footprints where the sand is damp. I am aware of the long straight line of shore, stretching toward Montauk, and I feel the wind at my back, I listen to the ocean and the gulls, I see the smoke trail of a freighter on the Atlantic. Of just such small things is emotion composed, and I will use them all later. When my heroine walks that particular beach, it will be as real for her as it was for me. Such impressions cannot always be photographed, and they go down in my notebook.

In this case the springboard of the human situation was a girl who had been adopted and whose adoptive parents had died. She must start out on what those who have been adopted call The Search. It is a search for her own being and heritage.

I had to do a great deal of research on adoption for this book, and much conjuring of ways in which to lead my heroine to East Hampton.

All the things I've been describing are done deliberately on the road to creating a story from empty white paper. But there is something else that enters in from time to time along the way. And this is the thing that is most difficult to explain to that non-writer. Yes, my dear Virginia, there *is* a Santa Claus. There *are* miracles.

One of them happened to me in an especially impressive way when I was working on *The Golden Unicorn*. Because the East Hampton scene is not all that exotic, I had to cast around in doing my research for any extras that might be useful. So I drove out to Montauk at the eastern tip of Long Island, saw the windswept little town, and the lighthouse on the point. I even arranged to visit the New York Ocean Science Laboratory before I came home. But how on earth was I to get any of this into my story?

I saw the problem coming while I was still in the plotting stage, and it had not cleared up by the time I was writing. It would be necessary to take five characters out to Montauk in order to use that setting. I needed that much more wordage in the story, I needed a gap when these characters would be away from East Hampton, and I wanted to use Montauk as a break from the East Hampton scenes. But how was I to do this? In a story, no moves can be made that have nothing to do with the plot. Travelogues are tiresome. There must be a reason to go, and something interesting must happen that will affect the story, affect the main problems that face the heroine. Only I couldn't think of a thing that would answer these conditions. Nothing.

From long experience I have learned that the most difficult of problems can be solved, that there is always a way. But I was getting very close to the Montauk scene in my writing, and I still hadn't the faintest idea of how I could use it. Finally, I gave up forward writing and went back to read the whole manuscript through from the beginning.

Harnessing the subconscious

On the day before I *had* to solve the problem, I lay down in the afternoon for a nap, and began idly to think about what I might do. And in that relaxed state, suddenly, without warning, I saw it, all there in my mind: A good scene, a dramatic and necessary scene, with a new character introduced whom I'd known nothing about moments before. No nap. I got right up and wrote it all down before it could escape, and the next day, I went to my typewriter and turned out one of the good, dramatic scenes in the book.

Call it the subconscious, call it Santa Claus, call it what you like, there is something there that goes to work on creative problems without conscious effort on the writer's part, and works out all the details when you're not even looking.

This wasn't the only time that happened to me. For the subconscious is something I use constantly in my writing, and it never fails me when I need it badly. In the case of *The Golden Unicorn,* it worked a little more spectacularly than usual. Nevertheless, I had taken all the right steps to bring about the solution. There are three: 1. Think about the problem and feed it into your mind. 2. Leave it alone and turn to other things. 3. After an interval, take it out and look at it. Usually, the answer will be there. If not, repeat the process.

The most interesting thing to me in this particular instance was the fact that everything in the solution was already buried in the body of what I had written. The setting of a particular house had been mentioned and the extra character planted, but never used. I hadn't been able to see the solution consciously, but when it all came to me in a flash, it was absolutely right. The new happenings grew out of everything that went before, and they led into what was to come. I now needed to go back and pull what was embedded to the surface, so that I could move the story along naturally to future happenings. But it took very little revision to do this.

On certain rare occasions when no trip at all was possible, I have done an entire background without visiting the scene. This was true of *Spindrift*. I had planned to visit Newport, Rhode Island, but illness and other difficulties intervened, so that I couldn't travel. The Newport Public Library helped me with lists of books I could read. The Newport Chamber of Commerce (another good source of information) sent me a packet of maps and brochures. My publisher sent me a marvelous book of photographs, and before I was through, I had walked all around Newport in my imagination. I also had the generous assistance of a library board member who lived in Newport and could keep me from making mistakes. The houses I used in the story were invented out of bits and pieces of reality, as the houses in my stories usually are.

There are still other springboards that can be used to give us any amount of story material when we are in that searching process. An interesting vocation will do it. Jobs, professions, exotic businesses are full of story material. So is almost any unusual human condition.

In one of my books for young people, *Secret of the Emerald Star,* setting isn't awfully important. The story could have been placed almost anywhere. I happened to use Staten Island, because that was where I was living at the time. My springboard was the subject of blindness. I wanted to write about a child who was blind. She wouldn't be my heroine, but would be a girl in whom the heroine became interested.

Through emotion to essence

Knowing nothing about blindness, I began first of all to read. But factual research is never enough. It is necessary to find a way to experience with your own emotions whatever it is you mean to write about. My first step was to visit a school in Manhattan where blind and sighted young people came together. The blind had their own homeroom, but they mingled with the others in moving about the school. Both groups got to know and accept each other.

I spent some time in that homeroom and talked with a number of blind children. One young girl was particularly outgoing, and it was she who introduced me to the world of the blind. I walked with her on the street, I went home with her and learned how she kept the possessions in her room so that she could easily identify colors, and distinguish whatever else she needed to know. But more than anything else, this girl gave me something I could feel and experience. Her own courage and lively interest in everything around her came through, and with her help I was made a rich enough person emotionally to write about a world I had known nothing about before.

The *essence* of a place, a person, a situation, is always what we must search for as writers. I remember sitting on a ruined wall in Camirus on the island of Rhodes in Greece—a town that Homer once knew. The ancient stones were as warm in the sun for me as for all those who had come before, and the pillars of the ruined temple as golden-white under the intensely blue sky of the Grecian isles. The distant sea was there as so many centuries had seen it before me; as I sat upon my wall, a small green lizard came out on the stones beside me. Only the lizard and I belonged to *now*. All this was *essence* that would later go into the books I set in Greece.

Where do ideas for stories come from? Where do they *not* come from? And how very enriching our search for these stories can be.

27

A LAYMAN'S GUIDE TO LAW
AND THE COURTS

WRITERS of suspense and mystery fiction will find the following information a valuable reference tool for use in describing points of law, courtroom procedures, criminal actions, legal transactions, and arrest procedures. This is a condensation of *Law and the Courts,* prepared by the American Bar Association.—*Ed.*

———

The processes of the law and the courts are baffling and mysterious to many laymen. The following material traces the steps normally involved in a civil case and in a criminal case, explaining the procedures common to most of them. It was prepared for use by nonlawyers (writers and others). The Standing Committee on Association Communications of the American Bar Association will, upon request, be pleased to offer assistance to writers in reviewing articles, scripts, and other material, for accuracy in legal procedure. The ABA Public Information Department also will be glad to help answer questions or direct inquiries to knowledgeable sources.

Some variations of procedure exist among the various state courts, and among the federal courts as well. When the occasion requires, details of procedure in particular courts, or in special

———

This chapter is a condensation of *Law and the Courts:* A Layman's Handbook of Court Procedures, and is reprinted by permission of the American Bar Association. The complete booklet is available for 50¢ from the American Bar Association, Circulation Department, 750 North Lake Shore Drive, Chicago, IL 60611. Copyright © 1974 by American Bar Association.

types of litigation, can be supplied by local attorneys, by court public information officers or other court officials.

Criminal cases

BRINGING THE CHARGE. Criminal charges are instituted against an individual in one of two ways:

1) Through an *indictment,* or *true bill,* voted by a grand jury, or
2) Through the filing of an *information* in court by the prosecuting attorney (sometimes called the county, district or state's attorney), alleging the commission of a crime.

In either case, the charge must set forth the time, date and place of the alleged criminal act as well as the nature of the charge.

In most states, crimes of a serious nature, such as murder or treason, may be charged by indictment only. In some states, the prosecutor has the option in any case to proceed by way of indictment or information.

THE GRAND JURY. The grand jury is a body of citizens (usually 16, but varying in number from state to state) summoned by the court to inquire into crimes committed in the county or, in the case of federal grand juries, in the federal court district.

Grand jury proceedings are private and secret. Prospective defendants are not entitled to be present at the proceedings, and no one appears to cross-examine witnesses on the defendants' behalf.

However, a witness before a federal grand jury is free to describe his testimony to anyone he pleases, after he leaves the grand jury room. To this extent, such proceedings are not secret.

Although all states have provision for impaneling a grand jury, only about half use it as a regular arm of law enforcement. In the others, the prosecutor, on his own responsibility, is empowered to make formal accusation of all, or of all but the most serious, crimes.

In states where the grand jury is utilized, it is convened at regular intervals, or it may be impaneled at special times by the court to consider important cases.

172 WRITING MYSTERY AND CRIME FICTION

The grand jury has broad investigative powers: it may compel the attendance of witnesses; require the taking of oaths, and compel answers to questions and the submission of records.

Ordinarily, however, the grand jury hears such witnesses as the prosecutor calls before it and considers only the cases presented to it by the prosecutor.

Nevertheless, a grand jury may undertake inquiries of its own, in effect taking the initiative away from the prosecutor. In common parlance, this is known as a "runaway" grand jury.

The grand jury's traditional function is to determine whether information elicited by the prosecutor, or by its own inquiries, is adequate to warrant the return of an indictment or true bill charging a person or persons with a particular crime. If the grand jury concludes that the evidence does not warrant a formal charge, it may return a *no bill*.

In several states, powers of investigation similar to those of the grand jury are conferred by law upon a single person, a judicial officer or a deputy appointed by him, known as a "one man grand jury."

ARREST PROCEDURE. When an indictment is returned by a grand jury, or an information is filed by the prosecuting attorney, the clerk of the court issues a *warrant* for the arrest of the person charged, if he has not already been arrested and taken into custody.

The law usually requires in a *felony* case (generally, a crime for which a person may be confined in the penitentiary) that the defendant must promptly be brought before a magistrate or justice of the peace (in federal cases, the U.S. Commissioner) and be permitted to post bond, in order to secure release from custody, and either request or waive a *preliminary hearing*. When the grand jury indicts, there is no preliminary hearing. In most states, however, persons charged with murder are not eligible for release on a bail bond.

Many jurisdictions permit law enforcement officials to hold a person without formal charge up to 24 hours for the purpose of investigation. But he may not be held for an unreasonable time unless a criminal charge is filed. In addition, the defendant formally charged with a crime is entitled to an attorney at all times. If he is unable to procure an attorney and if he requests counsel, the court will appoint an attorney to represent him, at public expense and without cost to him.

Special Note

Under the so-called Miranda decision of the United States Supreme Court, the following "basic Miranda procedure" and "typical Miranda statement given by an officer" are used:

I. Typical Miranda statement given by officer

Before we ask you any questions, you must understand what your rights are.

You have the right to remain silent. You are not required to say anything to us at any time or to answer any questions. Anything you say can and will be used against you in court.

You have the right to talk to a lawyer for advice before we question you and to have him with you during questioning.

If you cannot afford a lawyer and want one, a lawyer will be provided for you free of charge.

If you want to answer questions now without a lawyer present, you will still have the right to stop answering at any time. You also have the right to stop answering at any time until you talk to a lawyer.

II. Basic Miranda procedure

1. Warnings given *before* questioning a suspect who is *in custody* (custody = focus of interrogation + not permitted to move on).

2. Warnings always given when—
   a. subject is placed under *arrest.*
   b. interrogation in police *presence,* i.e., in station, or in squad car.
   c. if it is clear to officer that suspect thinks he has to answer.

3. Warnings not necessary for a mere witness (even grand jury witness who is not yet focus of investigation).

4. Warnings should be repeated after delay in questioning. Warning should be repeated when questioning officer changes.

5. Officer should immediately *stop* questions when suspect becomes silent *or* requests lawyer. If suspect agrees to talk and then goes silent, questions should stop.

6. Officer should give warning even to suspect who claims to make a statement that will show his innocence.

PRELIMINARY HEARING. If the individual charged with a crime requests a preliminary hearing before a magistrate, the court will set a hearing within a reasonably short time. At the hearing, the state must present sufficient evidence to convince the magistrate that there is reason to believe the defendant has committed the crime with which he is charged. The defendant must be present at this hearing, and he may or may not present evidence on his own behalf.

If the magistrate believes the evidence justifies it, he will order the defendant *bound over* for trial in the proper court—that is, placed under bond for appearance at trial, or held in jail if the charge involved is not a bailable offense or if the defendant is unable to post bond. The magistrate also may decide that even without bond the accused will most likely appear in court for his trial and therefore will release him on his *own recognizance,* that is, on his own promise to appear. If he concludes the state has failed to produce sufficient evidence in the preliminary hearing, the magistrate may dismiss the charge and order the defendant released.

ARRAIGNMENT. In most instances, a criminal case is placed on the court's calendar for *arraignment*. On the date fixed, the accused appears, the indictment or information is read to him, his rights are explained by the judge, and he is asked whether he pleads *guilty* or *not guilty* to the charge.

If he pleads not guilty, his case will be set later for trial; if he pleads guilty, his case ordinarily will be set later for sentencing. In cases of minor offenses, sentences may be imposed immediately. But in some states, arraignment and plea are separate proceedings, held on different days.

PREPARATION FOR TRIAL. As in civil cases, very careful preparation on the part of the state and the defense precedes the trial.

However, the defense may first enter a motion challenging the jurisdiction of the court over the particular offense involved, or over the particular defendant. The defense attorney also may file a *demurrer,* or motion for dismissal, as in a civil suit.

In preparing for trial, attorneys for both sides will interview prospective witnesses and, if deemed necessary, secure expert evidence, and gather testimony concerning ballistics, chemical tests, casts and other similar data.

Trials: civil or criminal

While in detail there are minor differences in trial procedure between civil and criminal cases, the basic pattern in the courtroom is the same. Consequently, this section treats the trial steps collectively.

OFFICERS OF THE COURT. The *judge* is the officer who is either elected or appointed to preside over the court. If the case is tried before a jury, the judge rules upon points of law dealing with trial procedure, presentation of the evidence and the law of the case. If the case is tried before the judge alone, he will determine the facts in addition to performing the aforementioned duties.

The *court clerk* is an officer of the court, also either elected or appointed, who at the beginning of the trial, upon the judge's instruction, gives the entire panel of prospective jurors (*veniremen*) an oath. By this oath, the venireman promises that, if called, he will truly answer any question concerning his qualifications to sit as a juror in the case.

Any venireman who is disqualified by law, or has a valid reason to be excused under the law, ordinarily is excused by the judge at this time. A person may be disqualified from jury duty because he is not a resident voter or householder, because of age, hearing defects, or because he has served recently on a jury.

Then the court clerk will draw names of the remaining veniremen from a box, and they will take seats in the jury box. After twelve veniremen have been approved as jurors by the judge and the attorneys, the court clerk will administer an oath to the persons so chosen "to well and truly try the cause."

The *bailiff* is an officer of the court whose duties are to keep order in the courtroom, to call witnesses, and to take charge of the jury as instructed by the court at such times as the jury may not be in the courtroom, and particularly when, having received the case, the jury is deliberating upon its decision. It is the duty of the bailiff to see that no one talks with or attempts to influence the jurors in any manner.

The *court reporter* has the duty of recording all proceedings in the courtroom, and listing and marking for identification any exhibits offered or introduced into evidence. In some states, the clerk of the court has charge of exhibits.

The *attorneys* are officers of the court whose duties are to represent their respective clients and present the evidence on their behalf.

The role of the attorney is sometimes misunderstood, particularly in criminal proceedings. Our system of criminal jurisprudence presumes every defendant to be innocent until proved guilty beyond a *reasonable doubt*. Every defendant is entitled to be represented by legal counsel, regardless of the unpopularity of his cause. This is a constitutional safeguard.

It is entirely ethical for an attorney to represent a defendant whom the community may assume to be guilty. The accused is entitled to counsel in order that he be protected from conviction on insufficient evidence, and he is entitled to every protection which the law affords.

JURY LIST. The trial jury in either a civil or criminal case is called a *petit jury*. It is chosen by lot by the court clerk from a previously compiled list called a *venire,* or in some places the *jury array.*

Many persons are exempted from jury duty by reason of their occupations. These exemptions differ from state to state, but in some jurisdictions those automatically exempted include lawyers, physicians, dentists, pharmacists, teachers and clergymen. In a number of others, nurses, journalists, printers, railroad, telephone and telegraph employees, government officials, firemen and policemen are among the exempt occupational groups.

On occasion, the qualification of all the jurors may be challenged. This is called a *challenge to the array* and generally is based on the allegation that the officers charged with selecting the jurors did so in an illegal manner.

SELECTING THE JURY. In most cases, a jury of twelve is required in either a civil or criminal proceeding. In some courts, alternate jurors are selected to take the places of members of the regular panel who may become disabled during the trial. These alternate jurors hear the evidence just as do the regular jurors, but do not participate in the deliberations unless a regular juror or jurors become disabled.

The jury selection begins with the calling by the court clerk of twelve veniremen whose names are selected at random from a box, to take their places in the jury enclosure. The attorneys for the parties, or sometimes the judge, may then make a brief statement of the facts involved, for the purpose of acquainting the jurors with sufficient facts so that they may intelligently answer the questions put to them by the judge and the attorneys. The questions elicit information such as the name, the occupation, the place of business and residence of the prospective juror, and any personal knowledge he may have of the case. This questioning of the jurors is known as the *voir dire.*

If the venireman expresses an opinion or prejudice which will affect his judgment in the case, the court will dismiss him for *cause,* and a substitute juror will be called by the court clerk. There is no limit on the number of jurors who may be excused *for cause.*

In addition to the challenges for cause, each party has the right to exercise a specific number of *peremptory challenges.* This permits an attorney to excuse a particular juror without having to state a cause. If a peremptory challenge is exercised, another juror then is called until attorneys on both sides have exercised all of the peremptory challenges permitted by law, or they have waived further challenges. The number of peremptory challenges is limited and varies with the type of case.

The jury is then sworn in by the court clerk to try the case. The remaining members of the jury panel are excused and directed to report at a future date when another case will be called, or excused and directed to report to another court in session at the time.

SEPARATING THE WITNESSES. In certain cases, civil or criminal, the attorney on either side may advise the court that he is *calling for the rule* on witnesses. This means that, except for the plaintiff or complaining witness and the defendant, all witnesses who may testify for either party will be excluded from the courtroom until they are called to testify. These witnesses are admonished by the judge not to discuss the case or their testimony with other witnesses or persons, except the attorneys. This is sometimes called a *separation of witnesses.* If the rule is not called for, the witnesses may remain in the courtroom if they desire.

OPENING STATEMENTS. After selection of the jury, the plaintiff's attorney, or attorney for the state in a criminal case, may make an opening statement to advise the jury what he intends to prove in the case. This statement must be confined to facts intended to be elicited in evidence and cannot be argumentative. The attorney for the defendant also may make an opening statement for the same purpose or, in some states, may reserve the opening statement until the end of the plaintiff's or state's case. Either party may waive his opening statement if he desires.

PRESENTATION OF EVIDENCE. The plaintiff in a civil case, or the state in a criminal case, will begin the presentation of evidence with their *witnesses.* These usually will include the plaintiff in a civil case or complaining witness in a criminal case, although they are not required to testify.

A witness may testify to a matter of fact. He can tell what he saw, heard (unless it is hearsay as explained below), felt, smelled or touched through the use of his physical senses.

A witness also may be used to identify documents, pictures or other physical exhibits in the trial.

Generally, he cannot state his opinion or give his conclusion unless he is an expert or especially qualified to do so. In some instances, a witness may be permitted to express an opinion, for example, as to the speed an auto was traveling or whether a person was intoxicated.

A witness who has been qualified in a particular field as an *expert* may give his opinion based upon the facts in evidence and may state the reasons for that opinion. Sometimes the facts in evidence are put to the expert in a question called a *hypothetical question*. The question assumes the truth of the facts contained in it. Other times, an expert is asked to state an opinion based on personal knowledge of the facts through his own examination or investigation.

Generally, a witness cannot testify to *hearsay*, that is, what someone else has told him outside the presence of the parties to the action.

Also, a witness is not permitted to testify about matters that are too remote to have any bearing on the decision of the case, or matters that are irrelevant or immaterial.

Usually, an attorney may not ask *leading questions* of his own witness, although an attorney is sometimes allowed to elicit routine, noncontroversial information. A leading question is one which suggests the answer desired.

Objections may be made by the opposing counsel to leading questions, or to questions that call for an opinion or conclusion on the part of the witness, or require an answer based on hearsay. There are many other reasons for objections under the rules of evidence.

Objections are often made in the following form: "I object to that question on the ground that it is irrelevant and immaterial and for the further reason that it calls for an opinion and conclusion of the witness." Many jurisdictions require that the objection specify why the question is not proper. The judge will thereupon sustain or deny the objection. If sustained, another question must then be asked, or the same question be rephrased in proper form.

If an objection to a question is sustained on either direct or cross-examination, the attorney asking the question may make an *offer to prove*. This offer is dictated to the court reporter away from the hearing of the jury. In it, the attorney states the answer which the witness would have given if permitted. The offer forms part of the record if the case is subsequently appealed.

If the objection is overruled, the witness may then answer. The attorney who made the objection may thereupon take an *exception*, which simply means that he is preserving a record so that, if the case is appealed, he may argue that the court erred in overruling the objection. In some states, the rules permit an automatic exception to an adverse ruling without its being asked for in each instance.

CROSS-EXAMINATION. When plaintiff's attorney or the state's attorney has finished his direct examination of the witness, the defendant's attorney or opposing counsel may then cross-examine the witness on any matter about which the witness has been questioned initially in direct examination. The cross-examining attorney may ask leading questions for the purpose of inducing the witness to testify about matters which he may otherwise have chosen to ignore.

On cross-examination, the attorney may try to bring out prejudice or bias of the witness, such as his relationship or friendship to the party, or other interest in the case. The witness can be asked if he has been convicted of a felony or crime involving moral turpitude, since this bears upon his credibility.

The plaintiff's attorney may object to certain questions asked on cross-examination on previously mentioned grounds or because they deal with facts not touched upon in direct examination.

RE-DIRECT EXAMINATION. After the opposing attorney is finished with his cross-examination, the attorney who called the witness has the right to ask questions on *re-direct examination.* The re-direct examination covers new matters brought out on cross-examination and generally is an effort to rehabilitate a witness whose testimony on direct examination has been weakened by cross-examination.

Then the opposing attorney may re-cross-examine.

DEMURRER TO PLAINTIFF'S OR STATE'S CASE, OR MOTION FOR DIRECTED VERDICT. At the conclusion of the plaintiff's or state's evidence, the attorney will announce that the plaintiff or state *rests.*

Then, away from the presence of the jury, the defendant's counsel may demur to the plaintiff's or state's case on the ground that a cause of action or that the commission of a crime has not been proven. In many states, this is known as a *motion for a direct verdict,* that is, a verdict which the judge orders the jury to return.

The judge will either sustain or overrule the demurrer or motion. If it is sustained, the case is concluded. If it is overruled, the defendant then is given the opportunity to present his evidence.

PRESENTATION OF EVIDENCE BY THE DEFENDANT. The defense attorney may elect to present no evidence, or he may present certain evidence but not place the defendant upon the stand.

In a criminal case, the defendant need not take the stand unless he wishes to do so. The defendant has constitutional protection against self-incrimination. He is not required to prove his innocence. The plaintiff or the state has the *burden of proof.*

In a civil case, the plaintiff must prove his case by a *preponderance of the evidence.* This means the greater weight of the evidence.

In a criminal case, the evidence of guilt must be *beyond a reasonable doubt.*

The defendant is presumed to be not negligent or liable in a civil case, and not guilty in a criminal case.

The defense attorney may feel that the burden of proof has not been sustained, or that presentation of the defendant's witnesses might strengthen the plaintiff's case. If the defendant does present evidence, he does so in the same manner as the plaintiff or the state, as described above, and the plaintiff or state will cross-examine the defendant's witnesses.

REBUTTAL EVIDENCE. At the conclusion of the defendant's case, the plaintiff or state's attorney may then present rebuttal witnesses or evidence designed to refute the testimony and evidence presented by the defendant. The matter covered is evidence on which the plaintiff or state did not present evidence in its *case in chief* initially; or it may be a new witness to contradict the defendant's witness. If there is a so-called *surprise witness*, this is often where you will find him.

After rebuttal evidence, the defendant may present additional evidence to contradict it.

FINAL MOTIONS. At the conclusion of all the evidence, the defendant may again renew his demurrer or motion for directed verdict.

The motion is made away from the presence of the jury. If the demurrer or motion is sustained, the case is concluded. If overruled, the trial proceeds.

Thus, the case has now been concluded on the evidence, and it is ready to be submitted to the jury.

CONFERENCES DURING THE TRIAL. Occasionally during the trial, the lawyers will ask permission to approach the bench and speak to the judge, or the judge may call them to the bench. They whisper about admissibility of certain evidence, irregularities in the trial or other matters. The judge and lawyers speak in inaudible tones because the jurors might be prejudiced by what they hear. The question of admissibility of evidence is a matter of law for the judge, not the jury, to decide. If the ruling cannot be made quickly, the judge will order the jury to retire, and will hear the attorneys' arguments outside the jury's presence.

Whenever the jury leaves the courtroom, the judge will admonish them not to form or express an opinion or discuss the case with anyone.

CLOSING ARGUMENTS. The attorney for the plaintiff or state will present the first argument in closing the case. Generally, he will summarize and comment on the evidence in the most favorable light for his side. He may talk about the facts and properly drawn inferences.

He cannot talk about issues outside the case or about evidence that was not presented. He is not allowed to comment on the defendant's failure to take the stand as a witness in a criminal case.

If he does talk about improper matters, the opposing attorney may object, and the judge will rule on the objection. If the offending remarks are deemed seriously prejudicial, the opposing attorney will ask that the jury be instructed to disregard them, and in some instances may move for a *mistrial,* that is, ask that the present trial be terminated and the case be set for retrial at a later date.

Ordinarily, before closing arguments, the judge will indicate to the attorneys the instructions he will give the jury, and it is proper for the attorneys in closing argument to comment on them and to relate them to the evidence.

The defendant's attorney will next present his arguments. He usually answers statements made in opening argument, points out defects in the plaintiff's case, and summarizes the facts favorable to his client.

Then the plaintiff or state is entitled to the concluding argument to answer the defendant's argument and to make a final appeal to the jury.

If the defendant chooses not to make a closing argument, which sometimes occurs, then the plaintiff or state loses the right to the last argument.

INSTRUCTIONS TO THE JURY. Although giving instructions to the jury is the function of the judge, in many states attorneys for each side submit a number of instructions designed to apply the law to the facts in evidence. The judge will indicate which instructions he will accept and which he will refuse. The attorneys may make objections to such rulings for the purpose of the record in any appeal.

The judge reads these instructions to the jury. This is commonly referred to as the judge's *charge* to the jury. The instructions cover the law as applicable to the case.

In most cases, only the judge may determine what the law is. In some states, however, in criminal cases the jurors are judges of both the facts and the law.

In giving the instructions, the judge will state the issues in the case and define any terms or words necessary. He will tell the jury what it must decide on the issues, if it is to find for the plaintiff or state, or for the defendant. He will advise the jury that it is the sole judge of the facts and of the credibility of witnesses; that upon leaving the courtroom to reach a verdict, it must elect a *foreman* of the jury and then reach a decision based upon the judgment of each individual juror. In some states, the first juror chosen automatically becomes the foreman.

IN THE JURY ROOM. After the instructions, the bailiff will take the jury to the jury room to begin deliberations.

The bailiff will sit outside and not permit anyone to enter or leave the jury room. No one may attempt to *tamper* with the jury in any way while it is deliberating.

Ordinarily, the court furnishes the jury with written forms of all possible verdicts so that when a decision is reached, the jury can choose the proper verdict form.

The decision will be signed by the foreman of the jury and be returned to the courtroom.

Ordinarily, in a criminal case the decision must be unanimous. In some jurisdictions, in civil cases, only nine or ten out of twelve jurors need agree to reach a verdict. However, all federal courts require a unanimous verdict.

If the jurors cannot agree on a verdict, the jury is called a *hung jury*, and the case may be retried before a new jury at a later date.

In some states, the jury may take the judge's instructions and the exhibits introduced in evidence to the jury room.

If necessary, the jury may return to the courtroom in the presence of counsel to ask a question of the judge about his instructions. In such instances, the judge may reread all or certain of the instructions previously given, or supplement or clarify them by further instructions.

If the jury is out overnight, the members often will be housed in a hotel and secluded from all contacts with other persons. In many cases, the jury will be excused to go home at night, especially if there is no objection by either party.

VERDICT. Upon reaching a verdict, the jury returns to the courtroom with the bailiff and, in the presence of the judge, the parties and their respective attorneys, the verdict is read or announced aloud in open court. The reading or announcement may be made by the jury foreman or the court clerk.

Attorneys for either party, but usually the losing party, may ask that the jury be *polled*, in which case each individual juror will be asked if the verdict is his verdict. It is rare for a juror to say that it is not his verdict.

When the verdict is read and accepted by the court, the jury is dismissed, and the trial is concluded.

MOTIONS AFTER VERDICT. Motions permitted to be made after the verdict is rendered will vary from state to state.

A *motion in arrest of judgment* attacks the sufficiency of the indictment or information in a criminal case.

A *motion for judgment non obstante verdicto* may be made after the verdict and before the judgment. This motion requests the judge to enter a judgment for one party, notwithstanding the verdict of the jury in favor of the other side. Ordinarily, this motion raises the same questions as could be raised by a motion for directed verdict.

A *motion for a new trial* sets out alleged errors committed in the trial and asks the trial judge to grant a new trial. In some states, the filing of a motion for a new trial is a condition precedent to an appeal.

JUDGMENT. The verdict of the jury is ineffective until the judge enters *judgment* upon the verdict. In a civil damage action, this judgment might read:
"It is, therefore, ordered, adjudged and decreed that the plaintiff do have and recover the sum of $1,000 of and from the defendant."

At the request of the plaintiff's lawyer, the clerk of the court in such a case will deliver a paper called an *execution* to the sheriff, commanding him to take and sell the property of the defendant and apply the proceeds to the amount of the judgment.

SENTENCING. In a criminal case, if the defendant is convicted, the judge will set a date for sentencing. At that time, the judge may consider mitigating facts in determining the appropriate sentence.

In the great majority of states and in the federal courts, the function of imposing sentence is exclusively that of the judge. But in some states the jury is called upon to determine the sentences for some, or all, crimes, In these states, the judge merely imposes the sentence as determined by the jury.

RIGHTS OF APPEAL. In a civil case, either party may appeal to a higher court. But in a criminal case this right is limited to the defendant. Appeals in either civil or criminal cases may be on such grounds as errors in trial procedure and errors in *substantive law*—that is, in the interpretation of the law by the trial judge. These are the most common grounds for appeals to higher courts, although there are others.

The right of appeal does not extend to the prosecution in a criminal case, even if the prosecutor should discover new evidence of the defendant's guilt after his acquittal. Moreover, the state is powerless to bring the defendant to trial again on the same charge. The U.S. and most state constitutions prevent retrial under provisions known as *double jeopardy* clauses.

Criminal defendants have a further appellate safeguard. Those convicted in state courts may appeal to the federal courts on grounds of violation of constitutional rights, if such grounds exist. This privilege serves to impose the powerful check of the federal judicial system upon abuses that may occur in state criminal procedures.

The record on appeal consists of the papers filed in the trial court and the court reporter's transcript of the evidence. The latter is called a *bill of exceptions* or *transcript on appeal* and must be certified by the trial judge to be true and correct. In most states, only that much of the record need be included as will properly present the questions to be raised on appeal.

APPEAL. Statutes or rules of court provide for procedure on appeals. Ordinarily, the party appealing is called the *appellant*, and the other party the *appellee*.

The appeal is initiated by filing the transcript of the trial court record with the appellate court within the time prescribed. This filing marks the beginning of the time period within which the appellant must file his *brief* setting forth the reasons and the law upon which he relies in seeking a reversal of the trial court.

The appellee then has a specified time within which to file his answer brief. Following this, the appellant may file a second brief, or brief in reply to the appellee's brief.

When the appeal has been fully briefed, the case may be set for hearing on *oral argument* before the appellate court. Sometimes the court itself will ask for argument; otherwise, one of the parties may petition for it. Often, appeals are submitted *on the briefs* without argument.

Courts of appeal do not hear further evidence, and it is unusual for any of the parties to the case to attend the hearing of the oral argument.

Generally, the case has been assigned to one of the judges of the appellate court, although the full court will hear the argument. Thereafter, it is customary for all the judges to confer on the issues presented, and then the judge who has been assigned the case will write an opinion. If a judge or judges disagree with the result, they may dissent and file a *dissenting opinion*. In many states, a written opinion is required.

An appellate court will not weigh evidence and generally will reverse a trial court for errors of law only.

Not every error of law will warrant a reversal. Some are *harmless errors*—that is, the rights of a party to a fair trial were not prejudiced by them.

However, an error of law, such as the admission of improper and persuasive evidence on a material issue, may and often does constitute a *prejudicial* and *reversible error*.

After the opinion is *handed down* and time for the filing of a petition for rehearing—or a petition for transfer, or a petition for *writ of certiorari* (if there is a higher appellate court)—has expired, the appellate court will send its *mandate* to the trial court for further action in the case.

If the lower court is *affirmed*, the case is ended; if reversed, the appellate court may direct that a new trial be held, or that the judgment of the trial court be modified and corrected as prescribed in the opinion.

The taking of an appeal ordinarily does not suspend the operation of a judgment obtained in a civil action in a trial court. Thus, the party prevailing in the trial court may order an execution issued on the judgment, unless the party appealing files an *appeal* or *supersedeas bond*, which binds the party and his surety to pay or perform the judgment in the event it is affirmed on appeal. The filing of this bond will *stay* further action on the judgment until the appeal has been concluded.

28 GLOSSARY OF LEGAL TERMS

accumulative sentence—A sentence, additional to others, imposed at the same time for several distinct offenses; one sentence to begin at the expiration of another.

adjudication—Giving or pronouncing a judgment or decree; also the judgment given.

adversary system—The system of trial practice in the U.S. and some other countries in which each of the opposing, or adversary, parties has full opportunity to present and establish its opposing contentions before the court.

allegation—The assertion, declaration, or statement of a party to an action, made in a pleading, setting out what he expects to prove.

amicus curiae (a-mī'kus kū'ri-ē)—A friend of the court; one who interposes and volunteers information upon some matter of law.

appearance—The formal proceeding by which a defendant submits himself to the jurisdiction of the court.

appellant (a-pel'ant)—The party appealing a decision or judgment to a higher court.

appellate court—A court having jurisdiction of appeal and review; not a "trial court."

arraignment—In criminal practice, to bring a prisoner to the bar of the court to answer to a criminal charge.

This list, which is a sampling of commonly used legal terms, is reprinted by permission of the American Bar Association from *Law and the Courts:* A Layman's Handbook of Court Procedures. The complete booklet is available for 50¢ from the American Bar Association, Circulation Department, 750 North Lake Shore Drive, Chicago, IL 60611. Copyright © 1974 by American Bar Association.

attachment—A remedy by which plaintiff is enabled to acquire a lien upon property or effects of defendant for satisfaction of judgment which plaintiff may obtain in the future.

attorney of record—Attorney whose name appears in the permanent records or files of a case.

bail—To set at liberty a person arrested or imprisoned, on security being taken, for his appearance on a specified day and place.

bail bond—An obligation signed by the accused, with sureties, to secure his presence in court.

bailiff—A court attendant whose duties are to keep order in the courtroom and to have custody of the jury.

best evidence—Primary evidence; the best evidence which is available; any evidence falling short of this standard is secondary; i.e., an original letter is best evidence compared to a copy.

bind over—To hold on bail for trial.

brief—A written or printed document prepared by counsel to file in court, usually setting forth both facts and law in support of his case.

burden of proof—In the law of evidence, the necessity or duty of affirmatively proving a fact or facts in dispute.

cause—A suit, litigation or action—civil or criminal.

certiorari (ser′shi-ō-ra′rī)—An original writ commanding judges or officers of inferior courts to certify or to return records of proceedings in a cause for judicial review.

chambers—Private office or room of a judge.

change of venue—The removal of a suit begun in one county or district, to another, for trial, or from one court to another in the same county or district.

circuit courts—Originally, courts whose jurisdiction extended over several counties or districts, and whose sessions were held in such counties or districts alternately; today, a circuit court may hold all its sessions in one county.

circumstantial evidence—All evidence of indirect nature; the process of decision by which court or jury may reason from circumstances known or proved to establish by inference the principal fact.

codicil (kod′i-sil)—A supplement or an addition to a will.

commit—To send a person to prison, an asylum, workhouse, or reformatory by lawful authority.

common law—Law which derives its authority solely from usages and customs of immemorial antiquity, or from the judgments and decrees of courts. Also called "case law."

commutation—The change of a punishment from a greater degree to a lesser degree, as from death to life imprisonment.

competency—In the law of evidence, the presence of those characteristics which render a witness legally fit and qualified to give testimony.

complainant—Synonymous with "plaintiff."

complaint—The first or initiatory pleading on the part of the complainant, or plaintiff, in a civil action.

concurrent sentence—Sentences for more than one crime in which the time of each is to be served concurrently, rather than successively.

condemnation—The legal process by which real estate of a private owner is taken for public use without his consent, but upon the award and payment of just compensation.

contempt of court—Any act calculated to embarrass, hinder, or obstruct a court in the administration of justice, or calculated to lessen its authority or dignity. Contempts are of two kinds: direct and indirect. Direct contempts are those committed in the immediate presence of the court; indirect is the term chiefly used with reference to the failure or refusal to obey a lawful order.

corpus delicti (kor'pus dē-lik'tī)—The body (material substance) upon which a crime has been committed, e.g., the corpse of a murdered man, the charred remains of a burned house.

corroborating evidence—Evidence supplementary to that already given and tending to strengthen or confirm it.

costs—An allowance for expenses in prosecuting or defending a suit. Ordinarily does not include attorney's fees.

counterclaim—A claim presented by a defendant in opposition to the claim of a plaintiff.

criminal insanity—Lack of mental capacity to do or abstain from doing a particular act; inability to distinguish right from wrong.

cross-examination—The questioning of a witness in a trial, or in the taking of a deposition, by the party opposed to the one who produced the witness.

cumulative sentence—Separate sentences (each additional to the others) imposed against a person convicted upon an indictment containing several counts, each charging a different offense. (Same as accumulative sentence.)

damages—Pecuniary compensation which may be recovered in the courts by any person who has suffered loss, detriment, or injury to his person, property or rights, through the unlawful act or negligence of another.

de novo (dē nō′vō)—Anew, afresh. A "trial de novo" is the re-trial of a case.

declaratory judgment—One which declares the rights of the parties or expresses the opinion of the court on a question of law, without ordering anything to be done.

decree—A decision or order of the court. A final decree is one which fully and finally disposes of the litigation; an interlocutory decree is a provisional or preliminary decree which is not final.

default—A "default" in an action of law occurs when a defendant omits to plead within the time allowed or fails to appear at the trial.

demur (dē-mer′)—To file a pleading (called "a demurrer") admitting the truth of the facts in the complaint, or answer, but contending they are legally insufficient.

deposition—The testimony of a witness not taken in open court but in pursuance of authority given by statute or rule of court to take testimony elsewhere.

direct evidence—Proof of facts by witnesses who saw acts done or heard words spoken, as distinguished from circumstantial evidence, which is called indirect.

direct examination—The first interrogation of a witness by the party on whose behalf he is called.

directed verdict—An instruction by the judge to the jury to return a specific verdict.

dismissal without prejudice—Permits the complainant to sue again on the same cause of action, while dismissal "with prejudice" bars the right to bring or maintain an action on the same claim or cause.

double jeopardy—Common-law and constitutional prohibition against more than one prosecution for the same crime, transaction or omission.

due process—Law in its regular course of administration through the courts of justice. The guarantee of due process requires that every man have the protection of a fair trial.

embezzlement—The fraudulent appropriation by a person to his own use or benefit of property or money entrusted to him by another.

eminent domain—The power to take private property for public use by condemnation.

enjoin—To require a person, by writ of injunction from a court of equity, to perform, or to abstain or desist from, some act.

entrapment—The act of officers or agents of a government in inducing a person to commit a crime not contemplated by him, for the purpose of instituting a criminal prosecution against him.

escrow (es′krō)—A writing, or deed, delivered by the grantor into the hands of a third person, to be held by the latter until the happening of a contingency or performance of a condition.

ex post facto (ex pōst fak′to)—After the fact; an act or fact occurring after some previous act or fact, and relating thereto.

exception—A formal objection to an action of the court, during the trial of a case, in refusing a request or overruling an objection; implying that the party excepting does not acquiesce in the decision of the court, but will seek to procure its reversal.

exhibit—A paper, document or other article produced and exhibited to a court during a trial or hearing.

expert evidence—Testimony given in relation to some scientific, technical, or professional matter by experts, i.e., persons qualified to speak authoritatively by reason of their special training, skill, or familiarity with the subject.

extenuating circumstances—Circumstances which render a crime less aggravated, heinous, or reprehensible than it would otherwise be.

extradition—The surrender by one state to another of an individual accused or convicted of an offense outside its own territory, and within the territorial jurisdiction of the other.

fair comment—A term used in the law of libel, applying to statements made by a writer in an honest belief of their truth, relating to official act, even though the statements are not true in fact.

false arrest—Any unlawful physical restraint of another's liberty, whether in prison or elsewhere.

felony—A crime of a graver nature than a misdemeanor. Generally, an offense punishable by death or imprisonment in a penitentiary.

forcible entry and detainer—A summary proceeding for restoring possession of land to one who has been wrongfully deprived of possession.

forgery—The false making or material altering, with intent to defraud, of any writing which, if genuine, might be the foundation of a legal liability.

fraud—An intentional perversion of truth; deceitful practice or device resorted to with intent to deprive another of property or other right, or in some manner to do him injury.

garnishment—A proceeding whereby property, money or credits of a debtor, in possession of another (the garnishee), are applied to the debts of the debtor.

gratuitous guest—In automobile law, a person riding at the invitation of the owner of a vehicle, or his authorized agent, without payment of a consideration or a fare.

guardian ad litem (ad lī′tem)—A person appointed by a court to look after the interests of an infant whose property is involved in litigation.

habeas corpus (hā′ be-as kor′ pus)—"You have the body." The name given a variety of writs whose object is to bring a person before a court or judge. In most common usage, it is directed to the official or person detaining another, commanding him to produce the body of the prisoner or person detained so the court may determine if such person has been denied his liberty without due process of law.

hearsay—Evidence not proceeding from the personal knowledge of the witness.

holographic will (hol-ō-graf′ik)—A testamentary instrument entirely written, dated and signed by the testator in his own handwriting.

hostile witness—A witness who is subject to cross-examination by the party who called him to testify, because of his evident antagonism toward that party as exhibited in his direct examination.

hypothetical question—A combination of facts and circumstances, assumed or proved, stated in such a form as to constitute a coherent state of facts upon which the opinion of an expert can be asked by way of evidence in a trial.

impeachment of witness—An attack on the credibility of a witness by the testimony of other witnesses.

inadmissible—That which, under the established rules of evidence, cannot be admitted or received.

in camera (in kam' e-ra)—In chambers; in private.

incompetent evidence—Evidence which is not admissible under the established rules of evidence.

indeterminate sentence—An indefinite sentence of "not less than" and "not more than" so many years, the exact term to be served being afterwards determined by parole authorities within the minimum and maximum limits set by the court or by statute.

indictment—An accusation in writing found and presented by a grand jury, charging that a person therein named has done some act, or been guilty of some omission, which, by law, is a crime.

injunction—A mandatory or prohibitive writ issued by a court.

instruction—A direction given by the judge to the jury concerning the law of the case.

interlocutory—Provisional; temporary; not final. Refers to orders and decrees of a court.

interrogatories—Written questions propounded by one party and served on an adversary, who must provide written answers thereto under oath.

intervention—A proceeding in a suit or action by which a third person is permitted by the court to make himself a party.

intestate—One who dies without leaving a will.

irrelevant—Evidence not relating or applicable to the matter in issue; not supporting the issue.

jury—A certain number of persons, selected according to law, and sworn to inquire of certain matters of fact, and declare the truth upon evidence laid before them.

grand jury—A jury of inquiry whose duty is to receive complaints and accusations in criminal cases, hear the evidence and find bills of indictment in cases where they are satisfied that there is probable cause that a crime was committed and that a trial ought to be held.

petit jury—The ordinary jury of twelve (or fewer) persons for the trial of a civil or criminal case. So called to distinguish it from the grand jury.

leading question—One which instructs a witness how to answer or puts into his mouth words to be echoed back; one which suggests to the witness the answer desired. Prohibited on direct examination.

libel—A method of defamation expressed by print, writing, pictures, or signs. In its most general sense, any publication that is injurious to the reputation of another.

limitation—A certain time allowed by statute in which litigation must be brought.

malfeasance (mal-fē′zans)—Evil doing; ill conduct; the commission of some act which is positively prohibited by law.

mandamus (man-dā′mus)—The name of a writ which issues from a court of superior jurisdiction, directed to an inferior court, commanding the performance of a particular act.

mandate—A judicial command or precept proceeding from a court or judicial officer, directing the proper officer to enforce a judgment, sentence, or decree.

manslaughter—The unlawful killing of another without malice; may be either voluntary, upon a sudden impulse, or involuntary in the commission of some unlawful act.

material evidence—Such as is relevant and goes to the substantial issues in dispute.

misdemeanor—Offenses less than felonies; generally those punishable by fine or imprisonment otherwise than in penitentiaries.

misfeasance—A misdeed or trespass; the improper performance of some act which a person may lawfully do.

mistrial—An erroneous or invalid trial; a trial which cannot stand in law because of lack of jurisdiction, wrong drawing of jurors, or disregard of some other fundamental requisite.

mitigating circumstance—One which does not constitute a justification or excuse for an offense, but which may be considered as reducing the degree of moral culpability.

moot—Unsettled; undecided. A moot point is one not settled by judicial decisions.

moral turpitude—Conduct contrary to honesty, modesty, or good morals.

murder—The unlawful killing of a human being by another with malice aforethought, either expressed or implied.

negligence—The failure to do something which a reasonable man, guided by ordinary considerations, would do; or the doing of something which a reasonable and prudent man would not do.

nolo contendere (nō'lō kon-ten'de-rē)—A pleading usually used by defendants in criminal cases, which literally means "I will not contest it."

objection—The act of taking exception to some statement or procedure in trial. Used to call the court's attention to improper evidence or procedure.

of counsel—A phrase commonly applied to counsel employed to assist in the preparation or management of the case, or its presentation on appeal, but who is not the principal attorney of record.

out of court—One who has no legal status in court is said to be "out of court," i.e., he is not before the court. For example, when a plaintiff, by some act of omission or commission, shows that he is unable to maintain his action, he is frequently said to have put himself "out of court."

panel—A list of jurors to serve in a particular court, or for the trial of a particular action; denotes either the whole body of persons summoned as jurors for a particular term of court or those selected by the clerk by lot.

parole—The conditional release from prison of a convict before the expiration of his sentence. If he observes the conditions, the parolee need not serve the remainder of his sentence.

parties—The persons who are actively concerned in the prosecution or defense of a legal proceeding.

peremptory challenge—The challenge which the prosecution or defense may use to reject a certain number of prospective jurors without assigning any cause.

plaintiff—A person who brings an action; the party who complains or sues in a personal action and is so named on the record.

plaintiff in error—The party who obtains a writ of error to have a judgment or other proceeding at law reviewed by an appellate court.

pleading—The process by which the parties in a suit or action alternately present written statements of their contentions, each responsive to that which precedes, and each serving to narrow the field of controversy, until there evolves a single point, affirmed on one side and denied on the other, called the "issue" upon which they then go to trial.

polling the jury—A practice whereby the jurors are asked individually whether they assented, and still assent, to the verdict.

power of attorney—An instrument authorizing another to act as one's agent or attorney.

prejudicial error—Synonymous with "reversible error"; an error which warrants the appellate court to reverse the judgment before it.

preliminary hearing—Synonymous with "preliminary examination"; the hearing given a person charged with a crime by a magistrate or judge to determine whether he should be held for trial. Since the Constitution states that a man cannot be accused in secret, a preliminary hearing is open to the public unless the defendant himself requests that it be closed. The accused person must be present at this hearing and must be accompanied by his attorney.

presumption of fact—An inference as to the truth or falsity of any proposition of fact, drawn by a process of reasoning in the absence of actual certainty of its truth or falsity, or until such certainty can be ascertained.

presumption of law—A rule of law that courts and judges shall draw a particular inference from a particular fact, or from particular evidence.

probate—The act or process of proving a will.

probation—In modern criminal administration, allowing a person convicted of some minor offense (particularly juvenile offenders) to go at large, under a suspension of sentence, during good behavior, and generally under the supervision or guardianship of a probation officer.

prosecutor—One who instigates the prosecution upon which an accused is arrested or one who brings an accusation against the party whom he suspects to be guilty; also, one who takes charge of a case and performs the function of trial lawyer for the people.

quash—To overthrow; vacate; to annul or void a summons or indictment.

quasi judicial (kwā'sī)—Authority or discretion vested in an officer, wherein his acts partake of a judicial character.

reasonable doubt—An accused person is entitled to acquittal if, in the minds of the jury, his guilt has not been proved beyond a "reasonable doubt"; that state of the minds of jurors in which they cannot say they feel an abiding conviction as to the truth of the charge.

rebuttal—The introduction of rebutting evidence; the showing that statements of witnesses as to what occurred is not true; the stage of a trial at which such evidence may be introduced.

redirect examination—Follows cross-examination and is exercised by the party who first examined the witness.

referee—A person to whom a cause pending in a court is referred by the court to take testimony, hear the parties, and report thereon to the court. He is an officer exercising judicial powers and is an arm of the court for a specific purpose.

rest—A party is said to "rest" or "rest his case" when he has presented all the evidence he intends to offer.

retainer—Act of the client in employing his attorney or counsel, and also denotes the fee which the client pays when he retains the attorney to act for him.

search and seizure, unreasonable—In general, an examination without authority of law of one's premises or person with a view to discovering stolen contraband or illicit property or some evidence of guilt to be used in prosecuting a crime.

search warrant—An order in writing, issued by a justice or magistrate, in the name of the state, directing an officer to search a specified house or other premises for stolen property. Usually required as a condition precedent to a legal search and seizure.

self-defense—The protection of one's person or property against some injury attempted by another. The law of "self defense" justifies an act done in the reasonable belief of immediate danger. When acting in justifiable self-defense, a person may not be punished criminally nor held responsible for civil damages.

separate maintenance—Allowance granted for support to a married party, and any children, while the party is living apart from the spouse, but not divorced.

slander—Base and defamatory spoken words tending to harm another's reputation, business or means of livelihood. Both "libel" and "slander" are methods of defamation—the former being expressed by print, writings, pictures or signs; the latter orally.

state's evidence—Testimony given by an accomplice or participant in a crime, tending to convict others.

statute—The written law in contradistinction to the unwritten law.

stay—A stopping or arresting of a judicial proceeding by order of the court.

stipulation—An agreement by attorneys on opposite sides of a case as to any matter pertaining to the proceedings or trial. It is not binding unless assented to by the parties, and most stipulations must be in writing.

subpoena (su-pē′nä)—A process to cause a witness to appear and give testimony before a court or magistrate.

subpoena duces tecum (su-pē′nä dū′sēz tē′kum)—A process by which the court commands a witness to produce certain documents or records in a trial.

summons—A writ directing the sheriff or other officer to notify the named person that an action has been commenced against him in court and that he is required to appear, on the day named, and answer the complaint in such action.

testimony—Evidence given by a competent witness, under oath; as distinguished from evidence derived from writings and other sources.

tort—An injury or wrong committed, either with or without force, to the person or property of another.

transcript—The official record of proceedings in a trial or hearing.

trial de novo (dē nō′vō)—A new trial or retrial held in a higher court in which the whole case is gone into as if no trial had been held in a lower court.

true bill—In criminal practice, the endorsement made by a grand jury upon a bill of indictment when they find sufficient evidence to warrant a criminal charge.

undue influence—Whatever destroys free will and causes a person to do something he would not do if left to himself.

venire (vē-nī′rē)—Technically, a writ summoning persons to court to act as jurors; popularly used as meaning the body of names thus summoned.

veniremen (vē-nī′rē-men)—Members of a panel of jurors.

venue (ven′ū)—The particular county, city or geographical area in which a court with jurisdiction may hear and determine a case.

verdict—In practice, the formal and unanimous decision or finding made by a jury, reported to the court and accepted by it.

waiver of immunity—A means authorized by statutes by which a witness, in advance of giving testimony or producing evidence, may renounce the fundamental right guaranteed by the Constitution that no person shall be compelled to be a witness against himself.

warrant of arrest—A writ issued by a magistrate, justice, or other competent authority, to a sheriff, or other officer, requiring him to arrest a person therein named and bring him before the magistrate or court to answer to a specified charge.

weight of evidence—The balance or preponderance of evidence; the inclination of the greater amount of credible evidence, offered in a trial, to support one side of the issue rather than the other.

willful—A "willful" act is one done intentionally, without justifiable cause, as distinguished from an act done carelessly or inadvertently.

with prejudice—The term, as applied to judgment of dismissal, is as conclusive of rights of parties as if action had been prosecuted to final adjudication adverse to the plaintiff.

without prejudice—A dismissal "without prejudice" allows a new suit to be brought on the same cause of action.

witness—One who testifies to what he has seen, heard, or otherwise observed.

writ—An order issuing from a court of justice and requiring the performance of a specified act, or giving authority and commission to have it done.

ABOUT THE AUTHORS

British mystery fiction writer CATHERINE AIRD's many crime novels include *The Religious Body, A Most Contagious Game, Henrietta Who?, A Late Phoenix, Slight Mourning, Parting Breath, Last Respects, His Burial Too, Some Die Eloquent, Passing Strange, The Stately Home Murder,* and *Harm's Way*—all Doubleday publications. *A Most Contagious Game* and *Henrietta Who?* were selections of the Mystery Guild. Ms. Aird lives in a small village near Canterbury, England.

JEAN L. BACKUS is the author of *Dusha* and *Letters from Amelia/An Intimate Portrait* and of three spy novels under the pseudonym David Montross. Her short mystery stories have been widely published here and abroad; one of them, "Last Rendezvous," was nominated for an Edgar Award by the Mystery Writers of America. Ms. Backus is a member of the National Board of Directors of the MWA and devotes much of her time to teaching writing at various writers conferences and to manuscript editing.

Short stories by CECILIA BARTHOLOMEW have been widely published in such magazines as *Ladies' Home Journal, Redbook, Woman's Day,* and *McCall's.* Her novels, *The Risk* and *A Touch of Joshua,* were both published by Doubleday.

REX BURNS is the author of six mystery novels featuring detective Gabriel Wager—the most recent one, *Strip Search,* was published in 1984. The first of these, *The Alvarez Journal,* was awarded an Edgar by the Mystery Writers of America as Best First Novel in 1976.

MAX BYRD, a professor of English at the University of California at Davis, is the author of three mysteries—*Fly Away, Jill, California Thriller,* and *Finders Weepers*—featuring detective Mike Haller. *California Thriller* was the winner of the 1982 Shamus award for "Best Paperback Original," given by the Private Eye Writers of America. He has also written nonfiction books, and serves as a consultant for the Squaw Valley Community of Writers.

STANLEY ELLIN is an internationally acclaimed mystery and suspense writer, whose novels and short stories have been translated into twenty languages. Several of his earliest novels have been recently reissued, including *The Eighth Circle* and *The Key to Nicholas Street.* Mr. Ellis was awarded the 1981 Mystery Writers of America Grand Master Award, his fourth Edgar Allan Poe Award to date. His latest novel, *Very Old Money,* a Book-of-the-Month Club alternate selection, was published by Arbor House. Several of his novels have been filmed by leading directors such as Alfred Hitchcock, Joseph Losey, and Clive Donner.

A prolific writer of mystery and detective fiction, LOREN D. ESTLEMAN has won wide acclaim for his Amos Walker private eye series, with such titles as *The Glass Highway, The Midnight Man, Motor City Blue, Angel Eyes,* and *Sugartown,* all published by Houghton Mifflin. His short mystery stories, which appear in such publications as *Alfred Hitchcock Mystery Magazine,* have garnered many prizes, including nomination for a Shamus Award given by Private Eye Writers of America. His novel *Kill Zone* (Mysterious Press) is the first in a new series introducing Peter Macklin. He writes with equal success in the western field, to which he has contributed such popular titles as *This Old Bill, The Hider, The High Rocks, Stamping Ground,* and *Aces and Eights* (all published by Doubleday), the last of these winner of the Golden Spur Award, made annually by the Western Writers of America.

ROSEMARY GATENBY's popular suspense novels include *The Third Identity, Whisper of Evil, The Nightmare Chrysalis, Deadly Relations,* and *The Season of Danger,* the last two Mystery Guild choices. Another, *Hanged for a Sheep,* was a Detective Book Club choice. Many of her novels have been brought out in paperback and translated into several languages. One of her short stories, "Revelation," was included in *Who Done It?,* an anthology edited by Alice Laurence and Isaac Asimov, published by Houghton Mifflin.

SUE GRAFTON is the author of two mystery novels, *"A" Is for Alibi* and *"B" Is for Burglar,* both published by Holt. *"A" Is for Alibi* was a main selection of the Mystery Guild. In addition to her two earlier novels—*Keziah Dane* and *The Lolly-Madonna War*—she has written short fiction, articles, nonfiction books, and, most recently, movies for television. These have included "Walking Through the Fire" (an adaptation of a book by Laurel Lee); "Sex and the Single Parent" (an adaptation of a book by Jane Adams); "Mark, I Love You" (an adaptation of a book by Hal Painter); and "Nurse" (an adaptation of Peggy Anderson's best seller), which went on to become a television series. Ms. Grafton and Steven Humphrey, her husband, wrote the pilot and served as story editors for the CBS television series "Seven Brides for Seven Brothers" and collaborated on three episodes. They also adapted two Agatha Christie novels for CBS television movies: "A Caribbean Mystery" and "Sparkling Cyanide" (written with Robert Malcolm Young); and a television movie called "Killer in the Family" (written with Robert Aller).

Author of ten novels and several nonfiction books, BILL GRANGER was awarded an Edgar by the Mystery Writers of America for *Public Murders,* the first of his "November Man" series, followed by the critically acclaimed *The British Cross* and *The Zurich Numbers,* all published by Crown Publishers.

Over the past ten years, suspense novel writer WILLIAM HALLAHAN has had six novels published, one of which, *Catch Me: Kill Me,* won the Mystery Writers of America Edgar. Mr. Hallahan writes, "Poe's ceramic bust with my name on it sits on my desk and watches me write."

PAUL HENISSART's espionage novels—*The Winter Spy, Narrow Exit,* and others—have been widely praised for their realistic backgrounds and authentic settings and details. His familiarity with the foreign locales he used in his books stems from his travels in Europe, the Middle East, Africa, and Central America. For many years he worked as a journalist, a contributing editor to *Time,* and as chief of Radio Free Europe's Vienna and Paris bureaus. Hence, the events in his fiction, dealing with international terrorism and spies, closely parallel actual events.

For two decades, CLARK HOWARD has specialized in writing books, both fiction and nonfiction, based on criminal episodes in the U. S. *American Saturday, Zebra, Six Against the Rock,* and *Brothers in Blood,* were all true accounts of crime; *The Killings* and *Mark the Sparrow* were fictionalizations of well-known cases. He is also the author of ten other books and more than 200 short stories, one of which, "Horn Man," was awarded the Edgar in 1981.

P. D. JAMES is a best-selling British mystery writer and creator of the "intellectual detective," Adam Dalgliesh. Her novels include *The Black Tower, An Unsuitable Job for a Woman, Innocent Blood, Death of an Expert Witness,* and *The Skull Beneath the Skin.* In the fall of 1984, Scribner's published three of her novels in one volume called *Trilogy of Death.* Often called the "literary successor to Agatha Christie," she was awarded the Silver Dagger by the British Crime Writers Association for outstanding mystery and suspense novels.

PETER LOVESEY is the author of ten crime novels and a number of short stories published in *Ellery Queen's Mystery Magazine,* as well as several TV scripts. His novels include *Wobble to Death,* winner of the British (Panther/Macmillan) £1,000 award for a first crime novel; *Waxwork,* which won the Silver Dagger of the Crime Writers Association of Great Britain; *The False Inspector Dew,* which won the Gold Dagger; and his most recent, *Keystone.* His Victorian crime novels served as the basis of the popular TV series on *Mystery!,* featuring Alan Dobie as Sergeant Cribb. Using the pen name Peter Lear, he also wrote *Goldengirl,* which was adapted as a feature film starring Susan Anton and James Coburn in 1979.

In 1975 he gave up his teaching career to write mysteries and television scripts full-time, all of which have dealt with murder. They have included poisoning by strychnine, cyanide, laudanum, morphine, and digitalis; electrocution, drowning, stabbing, gassing, shooting, allergy reaction, and manual strangulation. He comments wryly, "My school reports described me as a thoughtful child, but my teachers didn't know what I was thinking."

DAN J. MARLOWE is the author of 28 mystery/suspense novels, including *Flashpoint,* which was awarded the Edgar by the Mystery Writers of America as the best paperback mystery of the year. His short stories have been anthologized in *Best Short Stories of the Year* (Dutton), several *John Creasy Crime Collections,* as well as Alfred Hitchcock and Ellery Queen collections.

PATRICIA MOYES has written several popular mystery novels featuring Chief Superintendent Henry Tibbett of Scotland Yard: *Murder à la Mode, Death on the Agenda, Falling Star, Johnny Under Ground, Murder Fantastical, Death and the Dutch Uncle, Dead Men Don't Ski, Down Among the Dead Men, Many Deadly Returns, Season of Snow and Sins, The Curious Affair of the Third Dog, Black Widower, The Coconut Killings, Who is Simon Warwick?, Angel Death,* and *A Six-Letter Word for Death,* all published by Holt, Rinehart and Winston. *Murder by 3's* is an anthology of three of her novels, and nine of her books have been reissued as Owl Paperbacks, most recently *Death on the Agenda, Dead Men Don't Ski,* and *Murder Fantastical.* She has also written a children's mystery, *Helter-Skelter.* Her books have been translated into eleven languages, and many of them have been serialized in England, the United States, Canada, Holland, Germany, Brazil, and Italy.

MARCIA MULLER is the author of the popular mystery novels featuring detective Sharon McCone—*Edwin of the Iron Shoes* (McKay), *The Tree of Death* (Walker), and, under the St. Martin's Press imprint, *Ask the Cards a Question, The Cheshire Cat's Eye, Games to Keep the Dark Away,* and *Leave a Message for Willie.* In collaboration with mystery novelist Bill Pronzini, she has written *Double,* a novel in which Sharon McCone and Pronzini's Nameless Detective join forces. She and Mr. Pronzini have also co-edited a number of anthologies, including *Witches' Brew, Dark Lessons, Kill or Cure* (all Macmillan), *Chapter and Hearse* and *She Won the West* (both Morrow), and a book of reviews of mystery/suspense fiction, *1001 Midnights* (Arbor House).

Once one of the FBI's ten most wanted men, in recent years AL NUSSBAUM has been involved in a wide range of writing activities: He has been the Hollywood correspondent for a number of European magazines, a syndicated book reviewer, and TV writer for both live-action and cartoon programming, and he has written over a score of juvenile and educational books. He is a former regional vice-president of Mystery Writers of America and continues to write short fiction under a number of by-lines.

LILLIAN O'DONNELL is the author of several successful detective novels with female detectives. Her books featuring Norah Mulcahaney include *The Children's Zoo, No Business Being a Cop, Dial 577 R-A-P-E, The Phone Calls, Don't Wear Your Wedding Ring, Cop Without a Shield,* and *Ladykiller.* About her Mici Anhalt series, very different from the Norah Mulcahaney novels, she writes: "The concept of focusing on crime from the victims' point of view has been a kind of crusade for me for some time. I began to put the idea into my stories with *Aftershock* (the first of the Mici books), *Falling Star,* and *Wicked Designs.* At last police, prosecutors, and judges are coming around to the idea of putting the victim before the criminal." Her other novels include *Dive into Darkness, The Tachi Tree, Death of a Player,* and *The Face of the Crime.*

The 1981 publication of GERALD PETIEVICH's two novels in one volume—*Money Men* and *One-Shot Deal* (Harcourt Brace Jovanovich)—marked the successful merging of his two careers: U.S. Secret Service Agent and novelist. He has covered a wide range of intelligence activities, including counterfeiting investigations, surveillance, undercover work, which took him to all parts of Europe (with Interpol), Africa, and the Middle East.

Ten years ago when assigned to Paris, he enrolled in a creative writing class at the Paris-American Academy of Fine Arts, and began to write seriously, forcing himself to keep a daily writing schedule.

His fourth novel, *To Live and Die in L.A.,* was bought for production as a major motion picture.

Since 1958, when Ballantine Books published his first novel, a mystery entitled *The Bright Road to Fear* (which was awarded an Edgar by the Mystery Writers of America), RICHARD MARTIN STERN has sold twenty-three novels. These include *Flood, Snowbound Six, The Bridge, The Will,*

Power, Stanfield Harvest, and the record-breaking best seller, *The Tower,* on which the film *The Towering Inferno* was based. He has also had more than a hundred short stories, novelettes and serials published in major magazines. He is a past President of Mystery Writers of America and a member of the British Crime Writers Association.

MARY STEWART's reputation as a writer of suspense fiction was assured since the publication of her first novel, *Madam, Will You Talk?,* praised for her impressive storytelling skill and talent for creating moods through setting. This was followed by a series of what were called variously "modern Gothics" and "contemporary thrillers": *Nine Coaches Waiting, My Brother Michael,* described as "rich in action and suspense." In 1970, Lady Stewart moved her fiction back in time to Arthurian England in the first of her series of novels about Merlin, *The Crystal Cave,* followed by three other Merlin novels—*The Hollow Hills, The Last Enchantment,* and *The Wicked Day* (all published by Morrow). Most of her titles were major book club selections, in the United States and Britain.

Former New York City detective DOROTHY UHNAK has recreated the world of crime and justice in her best-selling novels, which include *The Bait, Policewoman, Law and Order, The Investigation,* and *False Witness.* She is the recipient of both an Edgar Award and a Grand Prix de la litterature policière. Ms. Uhnak credits her fourteen years of police service for the authenticity that is apparent in her novels: "It's great for a writer; as a cop, you gain entry into homes, lives, whole worlds different from your own."

British novelist MICHAEL UNDERWOOD is the author of over thirty crime novels, most of them published in the United States under the St. Martin's Press imprint. His most recent titles include *Death in Camera* (1984) and *The Hidden Man* (1985). Mr. Underwood draws on his long experience as a barrister on the staff of the Public Prosecutor in London for his authentic police procedure court scenes.

One of the world's best-selling novelists, PHYLLIS A. WHITNEY, now 81, has written more than 65 books: over thirty mysteries and career novels for young people, and numerous mystery and romantic suspense novels for adults, most recently *Dream of Orchids.* Several of her novels—*Rainsong, Vermilion,* and *Emerald* (all published by Doubleday)—were Literary Guild Dual Selections. Paperback sales of her adult novel, including *Domino, Spindrift, The Turquoise Mask,* and *The Stone Bull* (under the Fawcett Crest imprint) total more than 25,000,000.

A member of several writers' organizations, Miss Whitney has taught writing at New York University and Northwestern University. She is also author of *Guide to Fiction Writing,* published by The Writer, Inc.

REFERENCE BOOKS FOR
MYSTERY WRITERS

BARZUN, JACQUES, and TAYLOR, WENDELL HERTIG. *A Catalogue of Crime.* New York: Harper & Row, 1971.

BRIDGES, B. C. *Practical Fingerprinting.* Revised by CHARLES E. O'HARA, with a foreword by AUGUST VOLLMER. New York: Funk & Wagnalls, 1963.

CHAPPELL, DUNCAN, and FOGARTY, FAITH. *Forcible Rape: A Literature Review and Annotated Bibliography.* (National Institute of Law Enforcement and Criminal Justice, Law Enforcement Assistance Administration, U.S. Dept. of Justice.) Washington, D.C.: Government Printing Office, 1978.

CUNLIFFE, FREDERICK, and PIAZZA, PETER B. *Criminalistics and Scientific Investigation.* Englewood Cliffs, N.J.: Prentice-Hall, 1980.

DE FOREST, PETER R., GAENSSLEN, R. E., and LEE, HENRY C. *Forensic Science: An Introduction to Criminalistics.* New York: McGraw-Hill, 1983.

FOX, RICHARD H., and CUNNINGHAM, CARL L. *Crime Scene Search and Physical Evidence Handbook.* (U.S. Dept. of Justice, Law Enforcement Assistance Administration, National Institute of Law Enforcement and Criminal Justice.) Washington, D.C.: Government Printing Office, 1973.

GODDARD, KENNETH WILLIAM. *Crime Scene Investigation.* Reston, VA.: Reston Publishing Co., 1977.

HAGEN, ORDEAN A. *Who Done It? A Guide to Detective, Mystery and Suspense Fiction.* New York: R. R. Bowker, 1969.

HALL, ANGUS (ed.). *The Crime Busters: The FBI, Scotland Yard, Interpol: The Story of Criminal Detection.* London: Verdict Press, 1976.

KEATING, H. R. F. (ed.). *Whodunit? A Guide to Crime, Suspense & Spy Fiction.* New York: Van Nostrand Reinhold, 1982.

KIRK, PAUL LELAND. *Crime Investigation* (2nd ed.). Edited by JOHN I. THORNTON. New York: Wiley, 1974.

————. *Crime Investigation; Physical Evidence and the Police Laboratory*. New York: Interscience Publishers, 1953.

LAURIE, PETER. *Scotland Yard. A Study of the Metropolitan Police*. New York: Holt, Rinehart and Winston, 1970.

PENZLER, OTTO (ed.). *Detectionary*. Woodstock, N.Y.: Overlook Press, 1977.

SCHULTZ, DONALD O. *Crime Scene Investigation*. Englewood Cliffs, N.J.: Prentice-Hall, 1977.

SMITH, MYRON J. *Cloak and Dagger Fiction: An Annotated Guide to Spy Thrillers* (2nd ed.). Santa Barbara: ABC-Clio, 1982.

SÖDERMAN, HARRY, and O'CONNELL, JOHN J. *Modern Criminal Investigation* (5th ed.). Revised by CHARLES E. O'HARA. New York: Funk & Wagnalls, 1962.

STEINBRUNNER, CHRIS, and PENZLER, OTTO (eds.) *Encyclopedia of Mystery and Detection*. New York: Harvest/HBJ, 1984.